Policeman

Claude L. Vincent, Ph.D.

University of Windsor

 PUBLISHING LIMITED
Toronto · Vancouver · Calgary · Montreal

Canadian Cataloguing in Publication Data
Vincent, Claude L.
Policeman

Bibliography: p. 142
Includes index.
ISBN 0-7715-5735-3

1. Police.   2. Police—Social aspects.
3. Police psychology.   I. Title.

HV7921.V55   363.2   C79-094342-5

1 2 3 4 5 6 7 8 9 HR 82 81 80 79

Printed and bound in Canada

Contents

Preface v

Introduction 1

PART I   THE STUDY

Chapter 1   Theory and Method   9

Theoretical Orientation 9, Symbolic Interactionism 9, Occupational Socialization 11, Different Kinds of Policemen 12, The Participant Observer 13, Advantages of Participant Observation 14, Potential Pitfalls of Participant Observation 15, Coping with Difficulties of the Method 17, Variations in Methodology 19, Limitations of this Study 22

PART II   THE POLICEMAN'S OCCUPATIONAL ENVIRONMENT

Chapter 2   The Social Setting   28

The General Setting 28, The City 29, The Legal Context 30, Summary 31

Chapter 3   The Police Bureaucracy   32

Make-up of the Force 32, The "Ideal" Policeman 36, Inside the Bureaucracy—Getting Ahead: Promotion 38, The Value of Education 40, Getting Along: Peer Pressures and Role Models 42, Superiors as Role Models 50, Conflicting Management Styles 50, Television 54, Summary 55

Chapter 4   The Policeman and His Public   57

Reciprocal Expectations 57, Coping with the Public 59, Summary 60

PART III   INTERACTING WITH THE ENVIRONMENT

Chapter 5   The Impact of Stress Situations   64

The Nature of Stress 64, Coping with Stress 64, At School in the Streets 67, In the Courts 75, Summary 78

Chapter 6   Isolation   80

"I Feel Like I'm Branded" 81, Harassment 81, Choosing
Isolation 82, Isolation from the Family 85, Dependency on
the In-group 87, Summary 90

PART IV   THE POLICEMAN

Chapter 7   **The Policeman: Responses to the Occupational Environment   92**

Identification of Attitudes 92, Police Attitudes Towards the
Criminal Justice System—Capital Punishment 93, Gun
Control 94, Social Workers and Parole Officers 94, Law
Courts and Lawyers 95, Bail 97, Police Attitudes Toward the
Police Department—Innovation and Change 97, The Police
Association 97, Women Police 98, Cowardice 99,
Corruption 100, Use of Force 101, Police Attitudes Towards
the Public—The Public in General 103, Women 104,
Immigrants 106, Blacks 106, Bikers 107, Homosexuals 107,
Ex-convicts 108, Behavioral Tendencies 109, Acutely
Observant 110, Secretive 111, Hard and Cynical 113, Imper-
sonal and Decisive 116, The Suspicious Sceptical
Policeman 118, Summary 123

Chapter 8   **The Policeman: Identity Based on Occupation   125**

Concept of Occupational Identity 125, The Concept of Occupational Identity Applied to Other Professions 127, Special
Factors in Development of a Police Occupational Identity 128

Chapter 9   **What of the Future?   131**

Some Suggestions: Dispatching Information 131, Sharing
Information Among Shifts 132, Sharing Information Among
Officers 132, Upward Communication 132, Recruitment 133,
Screening Out Potential Misfits 133, On-the-job Training 134,
Special Reward System 134, Paraprofessionals 135, Know-
ledge of Social Agencies 135, Professional Development 135,
Counselling Wives 136, Public Relations 136, Police Bill of
Rights 137, Civilian Review Boards 137

Epilogue   138
Glossary of Terms   139
References—Bibliography   141
Index   148

Preface

This book is about socialization; specifically the process whereby an individual becomes socialized into or adapted to an occupational role and develops an occupational identity. It is the outgrowth of a long and close association with the rank and file of a medium-sized Canadian police force. The association began in a rather casual way, arising out of the simple desire of a teacher to relate better to a special group of students—policemen taking courses in sociology. Within a very short time this modest personal goal was transformed into a larger, more concrete, more specifically defined objective.

The opportunity was there to observe and to specify the social factors—cultural, institutional, communal, occupational and personal—in the policeman's environment which had a special impact on him. This having been done, the various factors could then be presented in a systematic interrelated way to try to show how they effected a significant resocialization of those who become professionally involved in law-enforcement.

Entry into any occupation involves a certain amount of resocialization of the individual in the sense of the imposition of and the acceptance of certain norms, values, attitudes and behavioral traits commonly associated with that occupation. For most occupations this resocialization is minimal and is operative only within the occupational environment. Most people can leave their occupations behind at the end of a day. For many others this is not possible. The various societal factors which we have already mentioned, along with the degree of their acceptance and internalization by the individual, combine to produce a person who is identified by others and who, more or less, identifies himself or herself by his or her occupation. This phenomenon is quite apparent with respect to certain professions, especially the ones labelled the *helping* professions.

The clergyman, the doctor, the teacher, find it difficult, in almost any social context, to escape identification with their occupations. There seems to be no "off the job" for them. They find themselves expected by others to respond routinely as father confessor, good Samaritan, concerned educator.

An assumption underlying these expectations would seem to be that they have accepted this identification of themselves with their occupations.

The police are a striking example of this phenomenon as we shall discover in the course of this book. And our observation of them leads not only to a better understanding of an occupational group of great importance in our society, but also to a better understanding of the complex process of socialization in general and of the process of socialization-on-the-job in particular.

As already indicated, my initial contact with the members of this police force took place in the classroom in the early seventies. At times an entire class might be made up of policemen; at other times they comprised only a minority. From the very beginning I could sense a certain wariness and resistance on their part. They seemed to know that much of my knowledge of the police was second-hand and that I really knew very little about their lives and daily problems.

The classroom contact developed very well, and soon I was offered the opportunity of observing at first-hand what members of the police patrol division encounter during the course of an eight-hour shift. I was invited to participate in on-the-job situations and often I would be present in the patrol cars on different shifts. As time passed I began to take on the role of a more formal observer as I watched the men deal with various situations; many of their calls could be classified as "routine," but there were also many situations filled with the potential for violence in which personal danger to the officer hovered in the background.

It soon became apparent that worthwhile results might come from sharing the police role, in a limited fashion, over an extended period of time. Gradually, certain questions arose as the police subculture became more familiar: What impact does this kind of work have on a man? How effective and lasting is the training that the young policeman undergoes? Is it the public that isolates the police, or do the police isolate themselves as a means of self-protection? Do the police see the world in an essentially different way than the rest of the public? Is a policeman's self-image constantly being changed by his work and experience, or is he set in his ways prior to his experience? Can some of the attitudes and behavior tendencies of a policeman be changed by intensive re-education and resocialization? What affect does police work have on the policeman's social and family life? These and other questions formed the basis for this research of the policeman's world.

As my involvement deepened, two other things happened. First, I began to see a strong group solidarity and a shared outlook among the men. Second, and perhaps even more important from the point of view of the researcher, attitudes of mutual trust and respect were developing; the police were beginning to see me not as a nuisance or as a critic, but as someone to whom they could relate their experiences, their thoughts, and their feelings. Moreover, as they realized my discretion could be counted upon, they began to talk about their personal lives, their families, and certain problems not directly related to their jobs. In short, there were present the circumstances prerequisite to a participant-observer study of the police, centring on the strong group solidarity and the shared outlook I had observed.

When the study was done and the original manuscript complete, the officers with whom I had worked made comments, and offered suggestions on the proper usage of police terminology.

Finally, we discussed again at great length their daily professional experience. Throughout this book I have tried to make the point that of all the factors involved these daily experiences on the job and in the streets were the most important, not only in the growth and shaping of these men as police officers and as private persons, but also for interpreting the policeman to himself and to others.

Many thanks are due for help in the preparation of this book.

First and foremost, I would like to thank my early mentor, Abraham Citron, who convinced me that this topic was worthy of analysis.

Also to the many unnamed policemen, including the Chief of Police, who made it possible to do the field work and who kindly explained their occupational subculture to me, I extend a heartfelt "thank you."

Gratefully, I acknowledge all those who read the original manuscript, made suggestions, provided their comments and insights: Don Stewart, Rudolph Helling, Seymour Faber, and Adolf Ehrentraut. And to Marge Tomusiak for not only her assistance in the early stages of the book but also for her support and encouragement during the final stages of completion.

I also would like to thank those who gave so generously of their typing skills: Mary Beth Haber, Mary Goundry, Pat Calwell and Nancy Konrad.

A special thanks goes to my editor and taskmaster, Conrad Wieczorek, who was of immense help in the planning and reorganization of this book. Whatever shortcomings there are, however, belong entirely to the author.

Acknowledgments

Symbolic Interactionism: Perspective and Method by Herbert Blumer©1969, reprinted by permission of Prentice-Hall, Inc., New Jersey.

American Journal of Sociology, excerpts by Herbert Blumer, reprinted by permission of The University of Chicago Press.

"Reconsidering the Police Role" by Clifford D. Shearing and Jeffrey S. Leon from *Canadian Journal of Criminology and Corrections*, Vol. 19, No. 4, October 1977.

Violence and the Police by William A. Westley©1970 The Massachusetts Institute of Technology, reprinted by permission of MIT Press.

City Police by Jonathan Rubinstein©1973 by Jonathan Rubinstein. Reprinted by permission of Farrar, Straus & Giroux, Inc., New York, and International Creative Management, New York.

Justice Without Trial by Jerome H. Skolnick©1966, reprinted by permission of John Wiley and Sons, Inc., New York.

Psychologist With a Gun by Harvey Schlossberg and Lucy Freeman©1974, reprinted by permission of Coward, McCann and Geoghegan, Inc., New York, and Scott Bartlett Associates, New York.

Introduction

The modern policeman has been the subject of a number of studies in recent years, especially in Great Britain and the United States. Social unrest, civil disturbances, the rise of Black political power in the United States, commissions of inquiry, increased emphasis on the rights of the accused, rising crime rates, organized crime and rapid technological changes in society, have focussed attention on the police.

Nowadays, the individual voter and taxpayer is quite conscious of the taxes paid for police- and fire-protection and other services. The mass media feature reports of the soaring crime rate, outcries against and investigations into police brutality, lawbreaking, corruption, and inefficiency. Even the renowned Royal Canadian Mounted Police have come under close scrutiny. As a result of this, taxpayers are more demanding and expect more from the police who are now making salaries that are competitive and compare favorably with those of other occupations.

The police, in their turn, find themselves called upon to react to more complex situations and to enforce the law, often having to use tools and methods that are outmoded. An increasing reliance on highly sophisticated equipment requires difficult adjustment by police personnel.

Police departments and politicians across the country are well aware of public demand for effective and honest police work and are seeking through a wide variety of means to upgrade their forces and to eliminate waste. A task force which was set up in the province of Ontario by the Solicitor General's office to investigate policing in all its various aspects and to make recommendations presented its report in 1975. With the advent of regional government across the province, additional pressures have been brought to bear on police forces, to reorganize and consolidate, to become more professional in carrying out their duties and to revamp outdated rules and methods of operation.

All of these new pressures and demands are increasing the stress that is part of everyday police work whether on the street, in the patrol car, or at headquarters. All of these factors have made the role of the policeman increasingly difficult. Difficult not only to take on, but difficult also to appreciate.

Sociologists in the area of work and occupations attempt, as one aspect of their work, to examine the process whereby an individual is socialized into an occupational role and develops an occupational identity. This book aims to analyse the process and the effect of socialization into the occupational role of policeman.[1]

In order to study how a policeman responds to his work situation, an analysis of his complex working environment is first required. One must select the features that, in the policeman's own eyes, have the greatest impact on him. It is only after viewing those situations with which the policeman has to contend, that one can hope to make some sense of his responses. As will be shown, this is a work environment that differs markedly from that of any other occupation. It is the main contention of this book that the circumstances of this occupation and the policeman's response to it have a major and lasting effect on the individual that is different in kind and degree from that of other occupations. To make this apparent, the book has been divided into four parts:

Part I, Chapter 1, presents the aims of this study, its theoretical orientation, and its methodology: why it was used, the results obtained, its problem areas and its limitations.

Part II deals with the more general aspects of the work environment in which policemen find themselves. Chapter 2 sketches the broad social, cultural, historical, and institutional framework which the police in our study share with the rest of their community.

Chapter 3, "Police Bureaucracy," explores one of the more immediate elements of the policeman's occupational environment. In this chapter, the police themselves are given an opportunity to voice their own perceptions of the structure, of rules and regulations, of their own roles and expectations, and of the persons with whom they must work.

As pointed out earlier, there has been, in the last two decades, much material published about the police. It has been written by former policemen, by sociologists, by criminologists or by psychologists who have spent anywhere from several months to a year observing various police forces, primarily in the United States. From these studies have come many different images of the policeman. At one extreme, there are a few angry exposés of the policeman as a uniformed thug with one hand involved in graft and the other brutalizing innocent citizens with gun, fist or club (Turner, 1968; Chevigny, 1969; Stark, 1972). This image is as much at variance with reality as its opposite, the infrequent portrayal of the policeman as altogether fair, kind, impartial, dedicated and enthusiastic (Hogan, 1971; Daley, 1974). These are stereotypes; the reality is that policemen fall anywhere along a continuum, with a majority somewhere in the middle (Westley, 1970; Buckner, 1967; Banton, 1964).[2] As a result of all this, many people have become instant experts; a certain mythology about the urban policeman has developed, reinforced by movies and by several popular television series. In the seventies, the fascination of the public, both young and old, has shifted away from the cowboy on the plains and the sheriff in the small town to the life of the urban cowboy, the big-city cop. Despite efforts at realism, the images projected are often very different from the world the policeman actually encounters on the job. As a result of these distortions, false expectations arise on the part of would-be policemen, and some police forces have difficulty in attracting and keeping qualified personnel, despite high wages and job security. Chapter 4 takes up this matter in discussing the reciprocal expectations and perceptions held by the police and by the public. Public views and the common stereotypes that the police feel the public hold with respect to the police are also a critical aspect of the work environment. And it is not so much the objective reality of the public's views about the police that is important; it is what the police *believe* that reality to be, their perception of it, that determines, to a great extent, their reactions.

Part II, then, sets the wider scene, dealing with various aspects of the policeman's work environment: the broad social context he shares with other members of his community, the criminal justice system whose agent he is, the police bureaucracy within which he functions, and, finally, the context of public opinion which, as the policeman perceives it, has a powerful influence on him. Each of these elements of his environment calls for adaptation on the part of the policeman, and each induces stress. However, in addition to these broad socializing forces, there are two other special factors in the policeman's life which influence him powerfully. Part III examines these two factors and the policeman's response to them.

Chapter 5 considers those situations which the police themselves believe to be the most crucial as they discover and develop their occupational identities. The varied responses to work in the streets are all part of the difficult learning process that the youthful cadet and constable must undergo. These situations and his responses to them make or break the policeman.

A further problem commonly seen among police is the sense of isolation. As his occupational identity assumes greater importance and depth, the police officer gradually comes to depend less on the larger society and more on a smaller group of people who have similar values, perceptions and interests: his fellow policemen. Chapter 6 discusses how and why the policeman becomes relatively isolated from society at large and often from his immediate family as well. As in few other occupations, police work lends itself to high levels, not only of tension and stress, but also to a degree of isolation that can be virtually incapacitating. To deal with the stress and the isolation that go with the job, the policeman may and often does resort to alcohol and drugs. These attempts at coping, in turn, produce additional strains: on his marriage (often resulting in divorce), on his health, and sometimes they end in suicide. The concluding chapters of Part III attempt to show the effect of all the socializing forces that have been singled out in the development of what can be called an occupational identity.

Chapter 7 concerns itself with the policeman's response to selected aspects of his occupation and analyses the many components contained in the process: internalization of a particular set of norms, transmission and reinforcement of attitudes and behavioral tendencies prevalent in the police subculture. Gradually, almost imperceptibly, the policeman develops an occupational identity through the internalization of the police occupational subculture. This resocialization takes place through daily interaction and activity with his fellow policemen and demanding encounters with the public.

Chapter 8 describes what is meant by the term, "occupational identity" and to what degree it applies to the police.

What of the Future?

The occupational life of the policeman is marked by alternating periods of boredom and crisis, of friendly camaraderie and harsh, stressful encounters. Very little has changed over the years with respect to this particular aspect of the profession. However, if factors in the work environment which contribute to the breakdown in health, morale or effectiveness of the police can be located or isolated, then change or improvement are possible. The most important part of any police force is its personnel. Rapid turnover, frequent illnesses and breakdowns, and low morale are indicators of frustration and dissatisfaction with certain aspects of the occupation; this frustration and dissatisfaction sometimes spill over into other areas of the policeman's life.

In his role as sociologist, an observer can analyse his data and sometimes locate problem areas in the group (in this case, in the occupation) he is studying. It seems evident, at least to this researcher, that positive, constructive recommendations can arise from this discovery. In presenting these the sociologist is changing roles and becoming an applied sociologist or social activist. Increasingly, however, students and the public are facing social scientists with the challenge to use the results of research in the shaping of public policy.

With this in mind, Part IV, Chapter 9, makes some proposals based on extended and careful observation of the police; their implementation could help to alleviate some of the problems and the ensuing frustration experienced by policemen. Most of these recommendations arose directly out of this study; others are the result of continuing contact with the police and represent what the police themselves feel might be helpful.

Notes

1. Throughout this book we shall be using the term "police*man*," since, at the time of the study, there were no women on the force. While many of the salient factors involved in the process of socialization may be the same for women as for men and while many of the outcomes may be the same, it would be the province of another special study to deal with the increasing number of women who are coming into the profession of law-enforcement.
2. For an extensive review of the literature on the police, see Lefkowitz, 1975.

PART I

The Study

Chapter 1

Theory and Method

Theoretical Orientation

The aim of this study of the police is to examine the process whereby an individual is socialized into an occupational role, develops an occupational identity based on that role's demands, and contributes to the maintenance or modification of its character. To do this, one focusses on what we can refer to as an occupational culture. Occupational socialization involves the internalization of this culture. The model used for this study has been shaped primarily, but not exclusively, by the theory of symbolic interaction.

Symbolic Interactionism

In studying human society, symbolic interactionists focus on the individual and on his relationships to other individuals *within a shared symbolic environment*. It is because people share the meanings of symbols (verbal or non-verbal)[1] that there is regularity in social behavior.

> Symbolic interaction involves *interpretation,* or ascertaining the meaning of the actions or remarks of the other person, and *definition,* or conveying indications to another person as to how he is to act. Human association consists of a process of such interpretation and definition. Through this process, the participants fit their own acts to the ongoing acts of one another and guide others in doing so. (Blumer, 1969: 66)

Symbolic interactionism conceives of social interaction as a dynamic process within which the individual is alert to changes within the situation and alters his responses as he evaluates the significance of these changes.

> As participants take account of each other's ongoing acts, they have to arrest, recognize or adjust their own intentions, wishes, feelings, and attitudes; similarly, they have to judge the fitness of norms, values, and group prescriptions for the situation being formed by the acts of others. (Blumer, 1969: 66)

People do not merely respond to stimuli nor do they blindly follow the norms and rules dictated by society. They assess and evaluate stimuli; they evaluate the adequacy of norms and rules, and they act on the basis of these interpretations and evaluations.

It is through the sharing of symbolic meanings that the individual is able not only to anticipate the actions of others, but able also to look upon himself as an object. The individual can "take the role" of another individual and see himself or herself from that other's perspective. For example, a person may become very angry with someone then later, after having tried to see the situation from the other's point of view, sees that his initial anger was really inappropriate. This discovery can lead to modification of behavior and perhaps, in this instance, to a spontaneous apology. Through this process, there develops a concept of self." We become objects to ourselves. We become angry with ourselves; we feel self-confident; we feel self-satisfied; we criticize ourselves, and our conceptions of ourselves change as we enter new environments, suffer defeats, achieve victories, have troubled consciences and the like.[2]

It was with this view of human interaction that my investigation of the policeman was undertaken. He is engaged in a process of interpretation and evaluation; he is alert to subtle changes in the interaction process; he modifies or possibly ignores rules as he adjusts to what are often extremely tense emotional encounters. He cannot be regarded as an unthinking automaton. On the other hand, the policeman's occupational role will necessitate restricting the ability to take on the role of the other in carrying out his duties. Just as the soldier in combat cannot very readily identify with the enemy nor a surgeon identify with the patient on the operating table, so the policeman cannot readily identify with a criminal in order to carry out his duties. The military socialize men to define the enemy as subhuman in order to prevent this empathy. Likewise, the surgeon will have the patient covered so that only that portion of the anatomy to be operated on is exposed. This is done in order to diminish, in a sense, the "humanness" of the patient so that he may begin his cutting. The policeman is faced with a similar problem and must develop mechanisms to inhibit this empathy. This restriction is even more necessary for the policeman because of the number of times when he may be in situations requiring coercion through the application of force or the law.

Occupational Socialization

From an interactionist perspective, occupational socialization involves the internalization of an occupational culture. Hughes defines this occupational culture as "*a set of collective representations*, more or less *peculiar* to the occupation and more or less *incomprehensible* to the community. . . . This [set of collective representations] is complemented by *an occupational code*." This occupational code has two elements: "prescribed activity" of the members with respect to each other and a "policy which represents [the occupation's] relations to the community within which [its members] operate" (Hughes, 1958: 11-12).

However, the character of any occupational culture (that is to say, particular ways of acting, thinking, feeling, and so on) can only be imperfectly transmitted to the beginner prior to his actual performance on the job. The period of training and initiation defines only partially and conveys only abstractions or generalities about the true nature of the work involved.

Later, established members of the occupation, functioning as *role models* will further the process of socialization by the way they present themselves in the work setting. In this way they concretely transmit the occupational content (duties and the manner in which they are to be performed). At the same time, these individuals also shape the direction of the rookie's socialization through their *collective evaluation* of his role performance. Whether it occurs in a profession like medicine (Becker, *et al*, 1961), or an industrial occupation like steel-rigging (Haas, 1970), these evaluations become a major mechanism of informal social control within the occupation.

A further major component of the socialization process and its continuation throughout the occupational career is the work setting itself. It is here that particular interpretations of the occupational role are developed. At times these may even be contrary to the general code and policy of the organization and involve what Geer and her associates have aptly called a "learning of the ropes" (Geer, *et al*, 1968: 209-233). A learning of those specific cultural outlooks that may be unique to a given setting but, nevertheless, are central components of the occupational identity of members in that setting, is required.

The process of occupational socialization cannot be studied primarily in terms of structures, job descriptions, or organizational regulations. These things certainly influence the conditions within which role performances occur, but they provide little insight into the actual content of the process as expressed in the patterns of daily situations, events and interactions, through which the occupational role is actually defined and modified. These are the main concern of this study.

Different Kinds of Policemen

It has already been pointed out that there is little doubt in the minds of most authors on the subject that there is a distinct police occupational outlook, although there are differences of opinion about the form the occupational outlook takes.

The views attempting to explain the reasons for this distinctive occupational outlook fall for the most part into two basic groups. Some writers maintain that certain personality types are attracted to the job; others claim that the policeman is formed on the job.

Some writers (Turner, 1968; Rhead *et al*, 1970; Stark, 1972; Symond, 1972; Lefkowitz, 1973) stress the self-selection process as well as the screening process in determining the police occupational outlook. They maintain that certain personality types, who are aggressive, conformist, authoritarian, and rigid are attracted to law enforcement and are selected by a screening board who themselves are made up of similar personality types.

They are what they are before they enter the profession and, once on the job, they reinforce each other in accentuating these characteristics, which are rewarded both by peer-group approval and by promotion. The more insistent writers in this wide-ranging school of thought (Turner, Stark) tend to over-generalize and to paint a quite negative picture of the average policeman. A caricature is presented instead of a portrait corresponding to life. They describe the policeman as brutal, sadistic, authoritarian, secretive, suspicious, oversexed, cynical, conservative, ignorant and using his job as an outlet for aggressiveness and violence.

The contrasting set of views holds that the occupation makes the man, regardless of what he is at the outset. Niederhoffer (1965), Skolnick (1966), Westley (1970), all argue that the police identity develops as a result of socialization in the police social system and not as a result of the prior socialization of the recruit. Various aspects of the job mold, shape, and form him into "the policeman." These formative pressures include the total occupational environment, the reality that he is faced with on the job the continuous pressures from his peer group, the demands of his superiors, the influence of the older, more experienced men on the rookies, the shift work, the danger, and the boredom and isolation. As time passes, he develops an increasing awareness of himself in the eyes of others. This self-image is the result, mainly, of encounters with certain selected groups in society, and of shared experiences and conversations with fellow police officers. This view of himself and of the world is intensified if he socializes only with other policemen and their families away from the job. This self-image and this world-view affect every decision and every evaluation and analysis of reality: they result in selective and biassed perception, intensely held attitudes, and beliefs which affect behavior both on and off the job.

However, there is possible a third point of view, the one put forward by this study. This point of view holds that the job does affect the man, depending on the personality, the motivation, the previous experiences, and intelligence of each policeman. Those who cannot survive, who drop out or quit for whatever reason, who don't even make it through the training period or don't pass the selection board, are of a different breed. Their departure tends to intensify the similarities in the remaining group, since the most deviant or alien personality types are weeded out or weed themselves out by selective attrition. Those who remain, nevertheless, represent a wide spectrum of personality types who work at a variety of positions within the major role and who react in different ways to the stresses and strains of their work. They are not merely automatic response mechanisms who react similarly and thoughtlessly to the formative influences of a deterministic occupational environment; on the contrary they act on and affect the social environment in which they work out their destiny.[3] They will share many attitudes and behavioral tendencies but at the same time they differ markedly on a wide variety of matters.

The Participant Observer

Given the fact that socialization into an occupation is an extended process, and given the importance of daily experience in this process, it became apparent that the most appropriate research method for the understanding of this process and its outcome with respect to the police would be that of participant observation.

There are two basic approaches in sociology for collecting, preparing, and analysing data for the study of social interaction. One approach, that of *participant observation*, aims at *understanding or insight*, involves a certain amount of *introspection* on the part of the researcher and includes in the data to be recorded not only the overt behavior of the subjects under study but also their *subjective experiences*, that is to say, what they thought or felt while acting. The method of *survey analysis*, on the other hand is favored by those who feel that the sociologist should limit himself to *observable facts* and avoid subjective interpretations of what the actor might think or feel. It is a technique which involves the *use of questionnaires, surveys, sociometric devices* and *other measurements* commonly defined as objective. Depending upon the kinds of problems or social situations to be studied, one method may be preferable to the other.

Advantages of Participant Observation

Since the theoretical orientation of this particular study is primarily that of symbolic interaction, it is important to point out some of the interactionists' criticisms of current methodological practices. Blumer states:

> There is no demand on the survey researcher to do a lot of free exploration in the area, getting close to the people involved in it, seeing it in a variety of situations they meet, noting their problems and observing how they handle them, being party to their conversations, and watching their life as it flows along. . . . Moreover, the scholar who lacks first hand familiarity is highly unlikely to recognize that he is missing anything. (1969:37)

Completeness of data requires intimate and extended observation of the subjects under study. Furthermore, Blumer feels that the concepts and propositions of symbolic interactionism are devised for the *direct examination* of the empirical social world (1969:49). It is important to note also that the methodology favored by symbolic interaction insists on the design of a model to fit that which is to be studied in the empirical world and not the other way around. No one particular method appears to satisfy all the theoretical approaches found in sociology today. Therefore Blumer cautions:

> Respect the nature of the empirical world and organize a methodological stance to reflect that respect. (1969:60)

It is the opinion of not only the symbolic interactionists, but of this writer as well, that the best way to study the empirical social world, at least initially, is to enter and participate in it.

Another of the strengths of this particular method is its *flexibility*. One must always be open to unforeseen but significant occurrences. Frequently, one discovers one thing when he is looking for another. The researcher must be always thinking, analysing, recording, and observing. He tries not to impose his views or biases on the social situation he is studying. Rather, he tries to *stand in the place of the others and to see the situation as they see it*, sharing their thoughts and feelings. If he is an effective researcher, he learns from the "real world" and the people in it who become, in a sense, his teachers.[4] As we have just stated, proponents of this method argue that the principal way to study social behavior and processes is to study it in a *natural setting* where people act, react, and interact with each other in a variety of ways and in different situations. The situations are not contrived, and the subjects are actively involved with each other in a natural setting. The longer the period of time that the observer is intensively involved, the more *opportunity* he has *to assess* the changes taking place as well as the subtleties of the various social processes that are operating in that particular setting. For those who regard human association as an ongoing process of interpretation of, and definition by, acts which have a subjective meaning, this method has great advantages in that it *allows a more sensitive, subtle and complete interpretation of the causes and meaning of interaction.* Nevertheless, participant observation is not without its pitfalls; most of them were encountered in the course of this study. And attempts were made to cope with them.

Potential Pitfalls of Participant Observation

Many critics of this method contend that the *presence of a known observer distorts the behavior of the subjects being studied.* The subjects, aware of his presence, may try to convey the impression they feel the researcher deems appropriate.

It is also *difficult to record events while one is observing.* This means that the observer must rely primarily on his memory and judgment when writing up his reports. Furthermore, many events of importance may occur while the researcher is off duty or is involved with one member of a group.

Since all information presented is screened through the eyes of the researcher, the *possibility arises that situations or events have been misinterpreted by the researcher*, thus making a portion of his research invalid. What one may be getting is data on the subjective experiences of the researcher and not on those of the subjects of study. It is difficult to avoid *personal bias* in the analysis. This seems to be a common problem encountered among researchers. Becker observes:

> . . . . We do not report everything we observe, for to do so would
> violate confidences and otherwise do harm. On the other hand, we
> must take care not to bias our analysis and conclusions. (1961:15)

Because of the mass of experiences, images and conversations over which the researcher has no control, it is very *difficult to be judiciously selective.* There is also the danger of the researcher becoming so immersed in and even overwhelmed by the amount of information that he has obtained that he fails to see what is pertinent and meaningful. Information that could have been developed and tested at a later date using more rigorous procedures may also be lost.

Finally, there is always the possibility that *the researcher* might become so involved with his subjects, to the extent that he becomes one of them, that he *loses his objectivity.* During the course of this research, the attempt was made to remain in the background as much as possible, inconspicuous and silent, but the pose of the uninvolved, relaxed, casual observer is difficult to maintain in the presence of the injured, the intoxicated, the disturbed, the angry and the depressed people encountered during a tour of duty. At various times during patrols with the police, there arose feelings of excitement, alarm, nervousness, anger, resentment, impatience, and concern as each new incident presented itself, and, frequently, there was boredom during long periods of relative inactivity. However, since there was not, as with the officers, personal responsibility, nor a gun nor a uniform, it was in no way possible to experience, with the same intensity, the feelings, emotions, and reactions of the officers. Having experienced somewhat the same situations, however, the observer gradually began to understand their reactions and even their overreactions in non-academic, non-controlled, non-laboratory situations. They were called upon to make difficult decisions instantly, under pressure, often with a less than sympathetic audience loitering nearby.

The participant observer is always faced with *the problem of deciding what to include in his presentation and analysis*. All organizations attempt to uphold an image to outsiders, and the local police force is no exception. Also, if this researcher included in his report everything that he had observed or the many confidences shared, he could possibly have created difficulties for individuals involved as well as the police force. Information, whose sources were impossible to disguise, or which could possibly have harmed innocent people, has been omitted.

A wealth of material accumulated by the time the field work had been completed so that initially the writer was almost submerged in facts, reactions and interpretations. What he missed or ignored, the relative importance that he attached to certain events, are all matters of his personal observational skills and judgment. Discussions with other sociologists and social psychologists continued during and after the field work to determine what valuable insights could be extracted from the data that might have been overlooked earlier. After the field work was completed, lengthy discussions with policemen of all ranks and from different cities helped determine what was to be included in the final write-up. A great temptation for participant observers is *to include all the exciting anecdotes and events regardless of whether or not they serve any analytical or demonstrative purposes*. (Some extremely fascinating data was left out of the final presentation because it served little if any sociological purpose.)

There is the distinct possibility that in this study the writer's *perceptions and analyses* of the police world were *influenced by the personal relationships formed* with certain officers. The observer shared in the occupational life of the group that he intended to observe: to what extent was he affected and resocialized into adopting their versions and perceptions of reality? To avoid injecting the researcher's own biases into the material every attempt was made to present the data from the patrolman's own point of view and in his own words. If the data is used merely to justify and support the preconceived opinions not only of this researcher but of his subjects as well, one may reasonably conclude that this particular study is heavily biassed. If, however, the researcher's experiences are used to present a more balanced and realistic view of police work to the reader, then one can submit that the study has maintained a degree of objectivity. It does not invalidate the conclusions presented. One sixteen-year veteran on the Toronto police force commented about the study:

You peeled us like a banana! I don't think this would be the best type of police book to show to a rookie. It might discourage him. I don't believe you made any effort to whitewash that particular police force. The problems are the same everywhere. Here in Toronto it is just on a grander scale.

As was previously mentioned, the participant observer method for this study was chosen because it seemed to be the most effective method used by previous researchers. What perhaps is lost in breadth of cases or statistical information was gained in real-life emotional experience on the job. It is difficult to do realistic research about this type of work in a sequestered, safe, laboratory surrounded by books and tapes.

Coping With Difficulties of the Method

Presence of observer distorting behavior of subjects: This problem did indeed arise. Reactions to the presence of this observer in a patrol car were interesting and varied. When the purpose of that presence was explained, and conversation initially turned on topics of the patrolmen's choice, the uneasiness on both sides diminished but never entirely disappeared. The presence of an observer changed the usual working environment within the confines of the police car and disturbed the arrangements and the type and form of communication between the police partners. But later the majority of the patrolmen indicated that they thought it was, at the least, a good idea that a person teaching about society should share in some way the reality of their job conditions. Initially, any questions asked were of a factual kind, putting the police in the role of teacher and the observer in the role of student.[5] When one of the men was out of the car for coffee or for other reasons, and the other officer was left alone with the observer, the topic of conversation frequently would change; sometimes to questions about the observer's work. Viewpoints might be shared that would not be mentioned in front of the other officer; but as soon as the other man returned to the car, the entire situation changed, and the conversation returned to more impersonal topics. The solid wall of secrecy and silence is seldom breached by an outsider and when it is, it is only for a short while. The other officer in the car is not only a partner who must be counted on for support when the occasion arises, he is also a competitor insofar as promotion is concerned and, thus, acts as a restraining influence on the other. Each tries to maintain a particular image in the presence of the other and seldom lets down his guard completely with anyone, including even his partner. Too great an openness with outsiders is frowned upon in all police departments, and it is the exceptional police officer who acts "differently" especially in the presence of other policemen. Because of this unwritten rule, the policeman in the patrol car limits his partner's conversational freedom, especially when an outsider is present.

The presence of an observer affected not only the conversation of the men but also their behavior. They readily admitted this themselves and in later episodes indicated that they might have reacted differently had they been by themselves. The difference, in most cases, would not have been crucial, for when faced with dangerous or trying situations they did not seem capable of reacting in any way other than what the situation called for and what their training and experience dictated. They appeared much more concerned with the problem at hand, and the individuals involved, than with a third party present.

The use of casual dress, a sports shirt and light jacket, helped to reduce the formality of the situation in the car, created fewer problems for the police and aided in their acceptance of an outsider. Whenever and wherever the police were called, whether it was to a disturbance at a tavern or a domestic call or any other of the various situations where their assistance was required, the author accompanied them, and entered the premises. The mere presence of a non-uniformed third party sometimes disturbed people to a surprising degree. When it seemed required, the officers usually explained the presence of the observer by saying that he was an inspector or a detective and this explanation usually satisfied the people involved. However, when bikers or youths were stopped for traffic violations, they were visibly unsettled by the presence of a third party without a uniform and repeatedly wanted to know what he was doing there and whether or not he was a policeman. They had clear-cut role expectations of the police but were disturbed to find someone else there because it added an unknown element to the situation.

Collection and organization of data: After each session in the patrol cars or at headquarters, the evening's events, including date, time, district, and personnel involved, were written up at home. At first the writer tried to remember every episode and every call as well as the main points of the conversation. Personal reactions and observations about the reactions and attitudes of the police were all written down, not necessarily in chronological order, but as each highlight came to mind. Split shifts were the hardest to remember because it meant being out on two or three different shifts in the course of an eight to midnight, and then a midnight to four shift. This meant several contact hours with four to six officers and sometimes a patrol sergeant. Gradually, over a period of time, note-keeping became more selective as accidents, domestic quarrels, lost children, became regular occurrences. The focus became more centred on the attitudes and opinions of the men as well as their reactions during the long hours that sometimes elapsed between calls. The notes taken the previous evening would be reviewed in the morning and any highlights that might have been missed the night before would be included. The anecdotes and conversations were paraphrased but an attempt was made to preserve as much as possible the flavor and emotion of the life situation.

As the number of reports increased certain parts of the reports came to be identified and collected under various headings. Sectional headings were developed, including everything from bikers, to boredom to particular sergeants' criteria for good or bad police work. The notes under these various headings were then transcribed onto cards and filed. Over a period of time a lengthy card catalogue was developed with information under each title filed alphabetically. These files were reviewed intermittently and attempts were made to note any trends or changes in the attitudes or behaviors of the men. One of the most difficult tasks was to attempt to identify evidence that pointed to definite similarities in attitudes and behavior traits and to try to understand and account for some of the infrequent differences.

Analysis and presentation of data: The final stage of the research involved the formidable task of making sense out of all the information obtained and presenting it in a logical, coherent and organized fashion. This is the most arduous task of all when one uses this type of methodology. The reality of the policeman's world does not always fit neatly into a logical, systematic format. When the researcher is faced with this problem he often is tempted to sacrifice somewhat the spontaneity and holistic nature of the particular world he is analysing and attempts to break it down into more manageable parts.

Variations in Methodology

The methodology used in this research is actually a synthesis of two methods which were adapted over time to fit the slowly developing aims of the researcher. Initially, it took the form of participant observation; the researcher, however, never actively participated in police work, but merely observed the police carry out their duties. During the initial phase of the field work, the researcher made innocent attempts to assist the police but was informed that, although his efforts were appreciated, he was not protected by law to do this and could possibly end up in serious trouble. To illustrate, one night we came upon an apparently intoxicated female and the writer began to help the police place her into the patrol car. The police immediately took over and later explained that, had the lady laid a complaint, the police would have been covered, but the writer would not have been. The writer, then, attempted to be as unobtrusive an observer as possible. This particular restraint helped to diminish any bias that his presence might create in the setting being observed.

Gradually, over a considerable period of time, the writer spent a great deal of time with various policemen in leisure-time activities and at numerous police-sponsored gatherings. Here, the method again was participant observation, but the writer was much more involved and took a more active part in these functions. It was during this time that the observer's ideas about the police socialization process developed. Toward the end of the period during which the field work was taking place, the researcher had the fortunate opportunity of teaching another class composed entirely of policemen. They were asked, as were the men in the patrol cars, to carefully reflect on their occupational role and whether it was their experiences and decision-making in the field that were the most important formative or socializing influences in their police careers. They were then asked to describe and analyse in detail the situations and encounters on the job that they felt had influenced them the most; those experiences which helped them grow and develop into the occupational role.

At this stage of the research we were moving into a more open-ended interview method in order to test some of the theories that had been formulated in the field. The policemen themselves reflected on the above-mentioned major hypotheses that the writer had arrived at during his long period of participant observation. Through detailed and selective self-reporting and analysis, they substantiated the writer's hypotheses. This method contains certain hazards since the police could easily create fictitious situations in order to present a good image of themselves to the researcher. But, as will be seen in subsequent chapters, they were quite candid, describing many of the mistakes they made and the inner struggles with which they had to contend. This is a problem with any interview method, but the danger of this occurring was minimized by the good rapport the researcher developed over several years with the police. They did not appear to be threatened by the ongoing discussions. Rather, they appeared to enjoy the opportunity of presenting their views in detail. In many instances they volunteered information and indicated how important certain problems or points of view were to them. Frequently, they admonished the writer to enter certain insights and comments into the study. They felt that this was crucial for a better understanding of their position. At other times they directed the writer to other policemen to obtain specific information and even paved the way with introductions and supporting comments. These courtesies proved invaluable because they opened doors and provided contacts and information that would never be forthcoming under other circumstances.

The type of research used in this study parallels the gradual development of insights in the observer. At first the writer hoped to understand the world of the policemen and the part they played in the criminal justice system. Gradually, he became more aware of the impact that this working environment had on the men. As he became better acquainted with many of the policemen, he was able to spend more time with some of them when they were off duty. Because of this additional, lengthy, in-depth participation outside of the work environment, the writer developed a growing insight into the involved personal and occupational world of the police. It was only at this stage of the research that the observer could ask himself probing questions about the police that seemed pertinent, and focus his attention on certain aspects of their occupational setting. It was fortunate that his prior teaching contacts with the policemen had prepared him to deal with a variety of personality differences among the men themselves.

As previously mentioned, the writer first encountered the police as students. Several classes were held and the writer encountered approximately one hundred and fifty policemen. This gave the writer an opportunity to synthesize his academic knowledge of the police with the world of experience as seen by these men. Only after many months of participant observation was the writer able to form theoretical propositions and come to realize more specifically what he was looking for. The focus centred on the sharing of a common outlook held by all of the policemen interviewed. It might manifest itself in different ways or in different words, but the message that emerged was essentially the same. The observer then attempted to see and understand what were the main formative influences in the occupational world of the police. A wide variety of personality types was encountered, from the loud and boisterous to the quiet and introspective individual. Yet, amidst the wide variation of personality types, there remained that solid wall of shared attitudes toward practically every subject broached, especially by an outsider. It seemed as though they answered in unison despite the fact they were met on separate occasions by the observer.

The study moved from an exploratory one to the much more limited focus of the process of police socialization and an attempt was made during the field-work phase to abstract the main influences affecting the police. They never assigned any particular weight to the factors that were presented to them but they agreed that they were important and finally gave the writer what they considered to be the most important learning experiences on the job. These extended and vivid anecdotes are considered by the researcher to be strong indicators that his assessment of the situation is accurate. Perhaps there are many other influences that shape the occupational outlook of the police that were ignored or not taken into account, but we will leave the work of discovering these to other researchers.

Limitations of this Study

This study, using a synthesis of methods, has several limitations which will be outlined in this section. When dealing with the police force, it is important to remember that even though the Chief of Police had given the writer both oral and written approval to go out on patrol and to spend time at headquarters, there remained an element of cautiousness and restrained acceptance to the presence of an outsider. Over time, however, this wariness decreased somewhat but never entirely disappeared. When the police were faced with the usual calls for assistance, they went about doing their work and seemed relatively unaffected by the observer's presence. Many of them broke minor police rules and regulations while the writer was with them, thus indicating that they had no intention of changing their behavior merely because this observer was with them. A few of them attempted to fool the writer but most were aware that he had been dealing with the police for quite some time and would not as readily accept deceptions. Even though there were some very obvious misstatements made on various occasions the writer made no attempt to argue or correct them.

Most observations took place in the patrol cars with the uniform division. There was limited access to the detective, traffic and special investigation divisions. Most contacts were with the rank-and-file and not with the higher administration. As a result, the data obtained are primarily an indication of the life of the front-line patrolmen and how they perceive their role. For the reasons mentioned above, this study in no way represents an organizational presentation of the total police force any more than Becker's study of medical students was a total analysis of a medical school. Concentration was on the actual daily carrying out of patrol duties attempting to ascertain what the impact of the occupational role is on the men over a period of time. A detective, a special investigator or an administrator are faced with somewhat different problems and stresses than those encountered by the patrolmen (although they all share the same overall bureaucratic police setting). In order to generalize one's findings to the entire police force it would have been necessary for the observer to spend equal amounts of time with members of each division. However the time spent off the job with police at various gatherings enabled the observer to become acquainted with men from all divisions and many ranks. All of these men at one time or another had been patrolmen and had experienced the same socializing influences into the role. It is suggested that all the men on the force share the general police outlook with slight variations stemming from differences in rank or the division with which they are presently connected. As they progress through their police careers there is much shifting from division to division creating a certain amount of cross-fertilization of ideas and outlook.

The presence of the observer affected people when we responded to various calls. They were often ill at ease or uncomfortable until the police explained the observer's identity. Some nights he was promoted or demoted in rank depending on the whim or mood of the patrolmen he was accompanying.

Because of the writer's inexperience, very subtle human dramas were no doubt ignored completely; but frequently his hosts and teachers for the evening clarified what had really happened. It is often very difficult to perceive situations through the eyes of others, and often we may question what our own eyes tell us. Blumer notes:

> Since action is forged by the actor out of what he perceives, interprets, and judges, one would have to see the operating situation as the actor sees it, perceive objects as the actor perceives them, ascertain their meaning in terms of the meaning they have for the actor, and follow the actor's line of conduct as the actor organizes it—in short, one would have to take the role of the actor and see his world from his standpoint. . . . It is unnecessary to add that the actor acts toward his world on the basis of how he sees it and not on the basis of how that world appears to the outside observer. (1969:73-74)

For instance on one occasion two bikers wearing out-of-town colors were stopped. They were questioned and their bikes were searched. Both of them remained quiet throughout the searching procedures. One of them, however, was much more nervous than the other. After the usual careful banter and typical routine behavior, the police sent them on their way. It was only afterwards that one of the policemen explained to me that he had recognized the nervous one as a former member of the police auxiliary. This biker was aware that the policeman had recognized him and was afraid that the officer would bring up his past connections with the police in the presence of the other biker. Unknown to either the observer, the policeman's partner, or the other biker, this former auxiliary member quietly thanked the officer for not giving him away. The richness of this episode would have been completely lost to the observer had it not been for the explanation which was given after the bikers had left the scene. Field investigators depend heavily on the knowledge and experience of their subjects and unless they establish a good rapport with them they may remain oblivious to what is actually going on.

Since promotion is rather slow in the city under study, the observer had many opportunities to travel with experienced veterans who added much colorful and insightful background material that clarified situations and helped the observer gain a better understanding of the interactions taking place.

One must be cautious when one attempts to move slightly beyond the data gathered in the field to make additional generalizations. The data does indicate, to the satisfaction of this researcher, that there is a shared occupational identity that develops over the years as the police are gradually socialized into the role. We also believe that the data indicates that this shared outlook is developed primarily on the job. Many important factors that contribute to this police occupational identity have also been deduced from the data and will be analysed in greater detail in subsequent chapters. This occupational identity involves both attitudes and strong behavioral tendencies that serve the policeman well while he is on the job.

There are also indications from the data that these behavioral tendencies, while helpful on the job, tend to be dysfunctional in family or social life. However, more research would have to be undertaken in order to fully support this. Even if it were possible to obtain reliable statistical data concerning all the policemen on the force and their families it would still be difficult to justify inferences about causal processes.

Further studies of other police forces using accurate statistical data might enable broader generalizations to be made. Furthermore, if data concerning other service occupations where occupational identities are developed were obtained, studies could be undertaken to learn the impact of these occupations on the personal lives of the people involved. The evidence presented in this study on the personal lives of the policemen is sketchy at best; although even with accurate statistical data all that might be indicated is that there is a high correlation between police work and the following three variables: alcoholism, divorce, and family disruption.

In the next chapter we will consider the social context in which the policeman operates, taking into account such variables as the geographical, cultural and historical setting in which the policeman carries out his duties.

Notes

1. Symbol is any word, action, gesture, or thing to which meaning is attached. We know what a boy means when he gives a rose to a girl. Language is the basic human symbol.
2. It should be noted that the "Iowa School" of symbolic interaction founded by Manford Kuhn conceives of individuals as possessing a "core self" which remains relatively unchanged.

This author inclines to what is referred to as the "Chicago School" and the ideas of Herbert Blumer. Blumer and the "Chicago School" of symbolic interactionism view the self as "dynamic," that is to say, as undergoing change as the individual interacts with the environment.

3. *Ibid.*

4. See Glaser and Strauss, 1967, for a discussion of grounded theory—the necessity to base theory on analysis of real-life situations.

5. This reversal of roles, however, was more apparent than real. The policeman, in his daily duties and contacts with the public, is frequently called upon to explain, to suggest, and to inform. The sociologist in this situation has to adapt to a whole new occupational world filled with actors who change daily—a necessary prelude to more insightful observation.

PART II

The Policeman's Occupational Environment

Chapter 2

The Social Setting

When a sociologist studies the human interaction that takes place in a society, he must take into account aspects of the social structure that have a bearing on, or affect the observed interaction of, the human beings involved. This is not to say that the elements of the social structure within which the policeman works out his occupational role are crudely deterministic. However they do profoundly affect and constrain the form, direction and outcome of a policeman's behavior and how he defines his role (Lindsmith and Strauss, 1968:5-10).

In this chapter the social structure or context within which the police carry out their duties will be described in some detail. How this structure affects the policeman and how he reacts to it will be pursued in subsequent chapters. We begin with the large canvas of the general cultural setting, referring briefly to the Canadian criminal justice system. We will also be looking at the city itself and, finally, the occupational and ethnic backgrounds of its residents.

The General Setting

The police with whom we worked carry out their duties and their relationships with the public within a very definite framework. They are Canadians, living in Canada, with a provincial jurisdiction and in a border city. They are bound by the laws of this country and they share in varying degrees the culture and moral orientation on which these laws and norms are based; this affects the way the public perceives the police and also the way in which the police perceive themselves. In a multicultural setting and in specific situations involving first generation immigrants there is a strong possibility of misunderstanding brought about by very different definitions of the situation. The differing cultural backgrounds limit the shared meanings of symbols both on the part of the police and on the part of the newcomer and cause difficulty in communication.

The City

The city in which these police work is a medium-sized Canadian city with a population of about 200 000 people, spread over an area of 80 km². The city proper has grown very little during the last twelve years, the population increasing by only 4 500. On the other hand, as in most other metropolitan areas, the surrounding suburbs have mushroomed. The year 1966 saw the annexation of large surrounding areas into the city. The population increased from 115 284 to 192 000 and the area increased from 24 km² to 80 km².

Were it not for its close proximity and economic ties to its American neighbor, this city would not be especially different from other cities—at least from the policeman's point of view. However, because of the high crime rate, and the difficult racial situation in the neighboring city, the Canadian police tend to believe that there is an overflow of criminal activity from the American city. Some high-ranking officers estimate, on the basis of arrest statistics and information at their disposal, that at least ten per cent of the crime committed in their city originates next door. They further indicate that the main crimes involving United States' citizens are the carrying of concealed weapons, breaking and entering, holdups, the passing of counterfeit United States' currency, and the smuggling, in both directions, of stolen goods. There are also many drug-related crimes and contract murders.

The Canadian police are very conscious of the crime situation across the border and they work closely with the neighboring police force. Veterans on the force estimate that their work is increasingly more dangerous as the use of firearms proliferates. They attribute part of this situation to the influence of the American city and, not surprisingly, they strenuously recommend more rigid gun-control laws in their own province. Because of their heightened awareness and natural apprehension the Canadians feel somewhat "undressed" if they go across to the sister city without their own service revolvers. The impact of the town's proximity is powerful. Some young Canadian officers related that they had driven around with their American colleagues on their days off for a "little excitement." They believed that the latter dealt with more serious crime in one day than they did in their own city during an entire week—a reaction to the periods of boredom that they experience on the job.

The 1971 Canadian census figures show great ethnic diversity in the population of the city, with at least 35 different groups represented. The British element, those of English, Irish, Scottish, and Welsh extraction, constitutes fifty per cent of the population. Those of French origin comprise approximately seventeen per cent. The remaining thirty-three per cent belong to various other ethnic groups: Italians nine per cent, Germans five per cent,

Ukranians three per cent, Poles two per cent. Not more than one per cent of the population is black, although at any one time in the downtown area the black population is increased by tourists and visitors from their neighbor city. This gives the impression that the permanent black population is much greater than it actually is. Small groups of Chinese, East Indians, Arabs and Filipinos also live within the city's boundaries, thus increasing the racial diversity of the city.

English is the language most commonly used at home by eighty-six per cent of the population. Five per cent of the population speak Italian. Among those of French extraction, only 6 000 or three per cent of the total population use French in their homes. Thus, the need for bilingual services in the city is not as acute as in other areas of the province. However, because of its actual ethnic and linguistic diversity the police and the court system still require considerable use of interpreters.

The city is heavily industrialized and heavily unionized, with a great degree of militancy among its members, whether they belong to the UAW, CIO, CUPE or the Teamsters. Consequently the policemen, who come predominantly from working-class backgrounds, tend to be more sympathetic toward the needs and problems of the working class.

The Legal Context

The police also perform their work within a criminal justice system based on a particular social structure. This includes factors such as: (1) the values that underly the Canadian criminal and civil justice systems; (2) the varying people (judge, Crown attorney, policeman, lawyer, criminal, warden, prison guard) and the varying rights dealt with in specific ways by the justice system; (3) the norms, rules, laws, and procedures peculiar to the justice system of Canada, the province and the city covering and affecting the conduct of those who have occupations within this system (of paramount importance in this case is the provincial Police Act); (4) provincial laws and municipal by-laws.

As a result of being a part of this criminal justice system the police cannot take the law into their own hands; they cannot change it or ignore it. They are its agents. They are expected to abide by the law and enforce it according to clear guidelines. Whether or not the police agree with the law is not supposed to affect the manner in which they carry out their duties. Their role in the system demands that, regardless of personal feelings or preferences, they see to it that the people abide by the laws. Furthermore they do not have the right, as do most other citizens, to publicly question and criticize the law.

Summary

In this chapter we have explored some of the broader aspects, the social setting, in which the policeman must operate. The local police are drawn primarily from the heavily unionized, blue-collar working class and tend to share similar views about labor relations, gender-role definitions, and other matters. Coming for the most part from British backgrounds, their views tend to coincide with the dominant societal views concerning power, influence and minority groups. The medium size of the city makes it difficult for the police to retain anonymity. This can be personally inconvenient; but at the same time it may work to their advantage as police because they can more easily familiarize themselves with the city and its inhabitants. Finally, the close proximity of a large American city with a high crime-rate makes the police, naturally, apprehensive about the degree to which that criminal influence will be manifested in their own city.

As we have seen, it should be of little consequence what the policeman's feelings toward them might be, only that his occupational role requires him to function within the confines of this setting. In the next chapter we will look at the structure of the police force, and the ways in which the policeman must come to terms with his superiors and his peers.

Chapter 3

The Police Bureaucracy

Make-up of the Force

In addition to the foregoing general geographical, cultural and institutional conditions which affect the policeman's world, there are a wide variety of shared factors in the internal structure of the police force which shape his perceptions of reality. He steps into a very clearly defined, highly regulated, spatial and temporal environment that he must accept and to which he must conform his behavior. He has a definite working district and is assigned certain hours of shift work; there are rules and regulations; there are procedures; there is the Criminal Code; there is the Police Act, and unwritten departmental codes that constrain most aspects of his work life.

This chapter presents a brief outline of the structure of the police force, and then discusses the ways in which the men themselves perceive, respond to, and are socialized into their immediate working environment.

Personnel

At the end of 1977 the police force numbered 376 actual police personnel and 49 civilian personnel, of whom the majority are of English, Irish and Scottish background. The police personnel are distributed among six different divisions: administration, central records, criminal investigation, special investigation, traffic, and uniform or patrol. The uniform division is the most numerous with 221 police or almost sixty per cent of the entire force. The personnel are further broken down by rank with the Police Chief, the Deputy Chief, seven Staff Inspectors, nine Inspectors, seven Detective Sergeants, sixteen Staff Sergeants, thirty-five Sergeants, forty-eight Detectives, and 252 Constables.

Most of the police divisions operate out of the first precinct or the downtown headquarters building. There is a second precinct, staffed by the uniform division in the east end of the city, and there was talk of a third precinct being planned in the west end, but nothing has come of it because

POLICE FORCE PERSONNEL DISTRIBUTION	CHIEF OF POLICE	DEPUTY CHIEF OF POLICE	STAFF INSPECTORS	INSPECTORS	DETECTIVE SERGEANTS	STAFF SERGEANTS	SERGEANTS	DETECTIVES	CONSTABLES	CADETS	SPECIAL CONSTABLES	TELECOM OPERATORS	SWITCHBOARD OPERATORS	CLERICAL	TOTALS
ADMINISTRATION DIVISION															
Chiefs Office	1	1												3	5
Personnel Office			1											2	3
Community Services				1											1
Planning and Research						1									2
Training and Stores				1			1		1						2
Intelligence Unit						1		2	1					1	5
Prosecution Office						1			3					1	5
Total Administration	1	1	1	2		3	3		5					7	23
CENTRAL RECORDS DIVISION															
Central Records Office			1			1						7		13	22
Bylaws, Licences, Summonses							1		1	6	1				9
Identification Branch							3	2	5						10
Total Central Records			1			1	4	2	6	6	1	7		13	41
CRIMINAL INVESTIGATION DIVISION															
Criminal Investigation			1	2	6			38		1				2	50
Youth Branch					1			8							9
Total Criminal Investigation			1	2	7			46		1				2	59
SPECIAL INVESTIGATION DIVISION															
Special Investigation			1			1	3		15					1	21
Drug Squad									4						4
Total Special Investigation			1			1	3		19					1	25
TRAFFIC DIVISION															
Traffic Division			1			1	3		21	6					32
Safety Patrol							1		1						2
Total Traffic Division			1			1	4		22	6					34
UNIFORM DIVISION															
Precinct Number One			1	5		5	15		131				4	1	162
Precinct Number Two			1			5	6		69						81
Total Uniform Division			2	5		10	21		200					1	243
TOTAL PERSONNEL	1	1	7	9	7	16	35	48	252	13	1	7	4	23	425

of financial limitations and other higher priorities. Until 1969, according to the Inspector in charge of personnel, the turnover on the force was very heavy (approximately 20 per year). In his estimation the main reason for this was low wages. Since that time turnover has been reduced to approximately six or seven people a year and this is attributed to improved wages and better working conditions.

1978 SALARY SCHEDULE

Effective January 1st, 1978

	RATE	
CLASSIFICATION	ANNUAL	BI-WEEKLY
STAFF INSPECTORS	$27 976.00	$1 076.00
	$29 189.00	$1 122.65
INSPECTORS	$25 549.00	$982.65
	$26 359.00	$1 013.80
STAFF SERGEANTS DETECTIVE SERGEANTS	$23 526.00	$904.84
	$24 335.00	$935.96
PATROL SERGEANTS DETECTIVES	$21 503.00	$827.04
	$22 314.00	$858.23
POLICE CONSTABLES		
First Class	$20 291.00	$780.42
Second Class	$18 673.00	$718.19
Third Class	$17 601.00	$676.96
Fourth Class	$15 776.00	$606.77

Two rates of pay are provided for all ranks above the rank of Police Constable. Personnel are promoted to a higher rank first in an acting capacity, but receive immediately the minimum rate of pay for the rank to which they have been promoted. After completing a probationary period of twelve months they are confirmed in that rank or reduced to a former rank. If confirmed, they will receive the top rate of pay. These salaries compare favorably with those of any other police force in Canada. Despite the inherent difficulties of the job there is no shortage of candidates.

Requirements for Membership

In order to become a police officer in this city a person must fulfil certain minimum requirements:

He or she must be a Canadian citizen or a British subject with no criminal record or past arrests. The applicant must be between the ages of 18 and 20 years inclusive if applying as a cadet, or 21 and over if applying as a probationary constable.

The male applicant must be 1.7 m (5′ 8″) tall without shoes, with his weight in proportion, but the minimum is 72 kg (160 pounds). Female applicants must be 1.6 m (5′ 4″) tall without shoes and weigh a minimum of 54 kg (120 pounds). All applicants must have 20/20 vision uncorrected, and be physically fit.

All applicants must have at least a grade 11 education with grade 12 preferred and proof of education must be supplied.

Applicants must possess a valid chauffeur's licence.

They must attend an In-Service training program and successfully complete the Recruit Training Course.

When openings on the force occur those who have received the highest ratings from the selection board are hired as probationaries.

Among applicants, preference is given as a matter of policy to inhabitants of the city. It is felt that since municipal taxpayers support the police force, these good-paying jobs should be made available first to residents of the city. Transfers from other forces are discouraged unless the persons involved and their families were natives of the city originally.

Selection Procedures

The Staff Inspector in charge of Personnel pointed out that they receive many letters from would-be applicants giving their reasons for wanting to join the force. These persons are called before a selection board made up of the Chief, the Deputy Chief and the Personnel Director. There they are graded on a variety of criteria. They are asked what they would do in a variety of hypothetical situations and to give their reasons for acting in a particular manner. The board tries to ascertain their goals and their degree of ambition. They try to determine whether or not the applicants are basically honest. They look for self-confidence but not over-aggressiveness. They try especially to determine whether or not the persons under consideration can act in a reliable fashion under pressure. Applicants do not as yet have to submit to a battery of pschological screening tests.

Young people who had had previous work experience were perceived by this personnel board to be better prospects than those who were just out of school and who were, perhaps, too naive and immature for the job. They also felt that higher education was no assurance of good judgment and reliability. Many university graduates had dropped out in the past; the administration felt that their views were too rigid, or that they found it difficult to accept the realities and the discipline that the job requires.

Training

Once accepted, the probationaries enter a course of training. This consists of two six-week periods conducted at the provincial police college. Here they learn the fundamentals of police work. When not attending the college probationary officers do ordinary police work under close supervision during an eighteen-month period of assessment and In-Service training.

The "Ideal" Policeman

There is within the police department a concept of what constitutes an ideal policeman; it is a part of department ethos. He must have common sense, good judgment, be able to take charge in crisis situations and, of course, display courage and bravery when the occasion demands. Although this view was shared by most policemen there were still very subtle differences among the men as to what constitutes an ideal policeman. These differences can be attributed to several causes: age, years of experience, the success or failure of men seeking promotions, and especially to differences in rank and specialization.

Go By the Book

One recently appointed detective pointed out that he had learned more in six months as a detective than during all his previous years on patrol. He now saw things quite differently and better understood the need for careful procedures and regulations. The sergeants and inspectors, because of their additional responsibility and greater access to information, came to view things rather differently than the average patrolman who, more often than not, possessed limited and sometimes inaccurate information. Sergeant R. stated:

Hell, all these rules and regulations are there for a purpose. It sort of creates uniformity, a sense of unity and teamwork. Those damn hot-shot urban cowboys who want to by-pass all the rules constantly, and run their own show, create more problems than they are worth. The ones who keep the rules and do a good job resent these fellows who watch too many television shows.

Don't Be a Dead Hero

Rubenstein has pointed out that:

> Every policeman knows there are no foolproof precautions that guarantee security. He knows there are times when he must accept risks that cannot be wholly calculated. He also knows there are men who are willing to do things he does not care to do, and if they are credited with heroics for bursting into a room to disarm a man with a shotgun, he does not consider them any less stupid or himself any less brave. But no man is too strong or too clever to avoid all situations that he cannot master. And one of the requirements of being a "good cop" in the opinion of co-workers is having the combination of skill and will to hold on while waiting for aid. There is no shame among policemen if a man is beaten or injured, unless it is attributable to a lack of courage or to an avoidable error. There is little praise for a man who displays great courage if he does so at the risk of his life and of others. The patrolman who cuts off a colleague by driving over a sidewalk and through a stop sign to make a pinch will find himself working alone or transferred if he persists. The downcast rookie, crowned by a brick on his first day on the street, fearing his career had been terminated before it began, was told unmistakably what lay ahead. "Don't feel so bad, kid. You're one of us now. But when you come back to work, maybe you'll remember to wear your hat when you get out of the car," his sergeant said. His success is measured by his capability in controlling people, but his failure is not measured simply by defeat —although defeat is always humiliating—but errors, failures to act when necessary, and an unwillingness to take the calculated risks that everyone who uses his body as a tool must finally accept as a way of life. (1973:301)

The younger man seems to feel a great pressure to prove himself in the eyes of his fellow police officers. He tries to maintain good relationships with the other men and with his immediate superior officers. He realizes that his life may depend on support from his fellow police officer who drives around for eight hours at a stretch in the police car. Yet at the same time this man is his competitor for promotions and advancement. Many of the men initially expect special recognition and quicker promotion for feats of daring and heroic exploits. The problem is that there are very few, if any, "battlefield promotions." The best these men can expect is the respect and admiration of most of their fellow officers. This seems to be quite important to them. Constable W. had this to say about the "aggressive type":

If the man is pushing very hard, bucking for a promotion, he will not only become very involved in a variety of cases and incidents, he will [also] seek out trouble and problems and leads, rather than sit back like a lot do and put in his eight hours. In so doing he's going to get into a lot of difficult situations where the odds are he will probably make a number of mistakes, both in judgment and procedures. Although, he will on the whole be doing real police work and his mistakes will be honest mistakes, he will tend to be looked upon as a bungler and lacking in judgment by his superiors. They ride herd on you and you better not make too many mistakes.

The Quiet Fellow

The sergeants and inspectors are not impressed by those they define as "loud mouths" or "hot rodders." Sergeant O. said:

I have a lot of problems with some of these greenhorns. They go in with both feet and their mouths flapping. They make dumb arrests sometimes because they can't handle it out on the street. They don't have a sufficient reason to make an arrest but they do anyway because the character is making them look poor out on the street. I tell them not to bring them in if it won't stand up in court. I'm not going to look stupid and have my men make a whole lot of dumb arrests. If they can't hack it, they better quit because they better not expect me to cover for them and their stupid decisions. They're usually the loud-mouthed ones anyway who are trying to cover up for their own insecurity. I'm much more impressed with the quiet fellows who do their job. I've been through it all and over the long haul these guys make the best policemen.

The foregoing statements indicate that what the department, as represented by the higher-ranking more experienced men, wants is quiet and capable efficiency and not extreme individualism. The younger men, however, tended to admire courageous and aggressive models.

Inside the Bureaucracy

Getting Ahead: Promotion

Promotion in this system is based on assessment with respect to five criteria with twenty points possible in each of the areas:

1) *Oral evaluation* based on an interview with the Chief, the Deputy Chief, and the Staff Inspector from the officer's division
2) *Seniority*—the number of years on the force as a permanent officer

3) *Written examination* covering various aspects of the law and police procedures and regulations
4) *Evaluation by three staff inspectors*
5) *Evaluation by sergeants*—traffic, patrol.

A perfect score is 100 and men who obtain the highest scores are next in line for promotions when the positions become available. Passage through the ranks is generally slow because of the very low turnover rate in personnel.

In assessing the promotion system an experienced officer said simply, with a smile, "It's the fairest one we've got." This does not mean, however, that it has been accepted enthusiastically by the men. A high-ranking officer felt that the promotional system tended to favor those who wrote examinations well, but who may not have been the most capable in on-the-job performance. It is for this reason, among others, that the system is subjected to much criticism.

Constable J. became rather vehement when he stated:

There are a hell of a lot of relatives who are working together in this department. There are some inspectors and sergeants who are sending in good reports and pushing their sons-in-law, cousins and nephews for promotion. It isn't what you know or do but rather whose relation you are that counts in this police force. I don't think it hurts to be Scotch or belong to the Legion either.

The subject of nepotism and family connections came up again and again. Unlike Chicago and New York, however, it was a case of being Scottish or English rather than Irish. Constable R. states:

To even get on the force, let alone get any promotion you have to have a dad or uncle pulling for you. I know all kinds of guys who tried to get on. They had the size and the education, but they didn't have the drag. It's pretty good paying now, you know. What's the alternative for a guy in this city with only grade twelve. It's either ——'s or ——'s. I think the morale is pretty bad for that reason. Only the "right" kind of guys get promoted. They're all pretty boys, well-dressed, well-spoken; they play the game and don't rock the boat. I'm not breaking my ass anymore. We all get the same paycheque at the end of the month.

Officers, well acquainted with the reality of the internal structure of the organization, put little faith in the formal promotional mechanism and felt that many other factors were involved. Constable M. said:

To do well in the police force almost requires total time and dedication to playing the game. The commitment is not necessarily to good service but rather heavy involvement with the internal political game. You have to spend a lot of time with the Police Association socializing with the police. The time and effort required for this, the conniving, the planning, tend to make it very difficult on the wife. She's left alone and is almost a widow. It really isn't worth it, and if I could get a reasonably secure job somewhere else with about the same pay, I'd leave tomorrow. But what the hell, what chance do I have anywhere else? Now that we're close to getting thirty and out, all the more reason for hanging in there.

This belief among the men that there was too much favoritism was the most common complaint encountered. On the other hand, senior officers discounted this and were convinced that, because of the more objective criteria, better men were being promoted than was the case in previous years.

One inspector thought that, while the promotion mechanism was fair, there was always a danger of distorted subjectivism when it came to evaluation. As far as the written examination was concerned, the ratings are quite objective, since precise factual material is required; but sergeants and inspectors found it rather difficult to give the required personal evaluations of the men, especially when, in some instances, they did not know them too well. Inspector L. exclaimed:

How can I give a constable a real low mark for appearance? He may be pot-bellied and dragging his butt physically, but he still has his shoes shined, his hair trimmed, and his uniform is clean. These guys are really on their toes around evaluation time, but take it as a personal affront if they are given a low evaluation. Maybe a completely objective system would be preferable. It would make my job less painful and I would sleep better.

Over the years I have found a fair amount of unanimity among superior officers who were rating individuals. There may be small differences of opinion, or personality clashes, but on the whole a person gradually acquires a reputation on the force and he has to live with it. Some do change over the years and seem to mature into dependable guys. Others remain smart-asses and bellyachers all their life and whine about favoritism. Shit, they won't even write the exams after a while. What can you do to get these guys going? They just don't seem to have any drive; they put in their eight hours; but that's it. It's too bad we can't get rid of some of the malcontents but the Police Association makes it almost impossible.

The Value of Education: Intragroup Competition

In any organization there are always different factions contending for power, privilege and status; the police are no exception. Within this department, the biggest split into factions is that between the veterans, most of whom do not have much formal education, and the new men who are now required to have finished at least grade eleven high school.

As the criteria for promotion change, the older men feel additional stress and react adversely to the changes in the rules. It is occurring in every occupation where credentials are becoming more important. An increasing number of police have some or all years of their undergraduate work completed, and they are often the targets of rather harsh comments from the "old guard." Their mistakes are magnified, their judgment and common sense are questioned, and they are constantly reminded that bravery and good judgment are not learned in school but are qualities acquired and developed only through experience. This is the reaction of people fearful of being by-passed in the promotions by "young upstarts" who may be able to write examinations better but who are still "wet behind the ears," who need the seasoning which comes from practical experience.

Sergeants complain that the younger men, especially those with higher education, are always questioning orders and routines and seeking more responsibility in decision-making. One staff inspector pinpointed certain problem areas:

There is a group of guys who came in a few years ago who just seem to have all the questions and no answers. They don't take orders too well and wonder about everything. I guess they are products of the ultra-liberal permissive time. Thank goodness the new ones are easier to handle. Knock on wood!

Many of the older men, with experience in the armed forces and accustomed to giving and taking orders in accordance with standard military discipline, do not display this inquisitiveness and do not therefore present as great a problem of discipline for the sergeants.

Some of the men with more years in school have indicated, themselves, that their more extensive education has been a hindrance instead of a help on the job. Almost in echo of their elders and superiors, they reported that the knowledge acquired at university was not much help in the streets in stress situations. In many difficult situations book knowledge is by-passed in favor of instinct, sharp judgment and courage.

The younger policemen with more education find the long hours of relative inactivity on the job boring and come to see their education as no real advantage in the promotional scheme of things, especially with respect to the evaluations given by inspectors and sergeants. As a result of the slow promotions, the frustrations in being confronted with apparently senseless regulations, and the pointed, cruel humor from those with less formal education, some of the men with university training have resigned from the force. They feel that only lip-service has been paid to education in the form of a five hundred dollar increment to those with a university degree. What is actually taking place, they feel, is a rear-guard protective and delaying tactic by older, more experienced men who, worried about being passed over, are strongly opposed to any change in the system that would undercut their vested interests. Comments by men in middle and higher management seem to confirm this impression. Sergeant L. asserted:

We're not running an academic greenhouse here for intellectual nitwits and pansies. This is a police force and, by damn, we first and foremost need men with balls. My most dependable men are not those with the most formal education. They are the ones who, day in, day out, over the long haul, make the good decisions, the good arrests, and can work with a little teamwork.

Another night this same sergeant stated:

I find that there is a trend among younger policemen not to be so willing to risk injury by getting into fights. They are a little softer and tend to depend a little too much on the gun or the club. In my day if you didn't want to fight, or couldn't, you didn't last long because it got around fast. I think they have too much education and haven't had it as hard as we did. These guys want to avoid involvement and protect their job. They are very security-conscious, which is understandable. There aren't too many desk jobs available for them if they get badly injured on the job, so many of them play it safe. Maybe if they were sure that they would get a full disability pension if seriously incapacitated in the line of duty, they might be willing to mix it a little more.

Getting Along: Peer Pressures and Role Models in Police Work

The influence of the *peer group* is pervasive. His peer group of fellow constables becomes, in a sense, the policeman's occupational family, his new brothers, his main reference group. He will identify with them, tend to adopt their outlooks and see himself from the perspective of this new, all-important, reference group.[1] His peer group, initially, will be made up of men who hold the same rank and who are approximately the same age. Friendship patterns might cut across rank; but this only happens when he is off duty. Most of the men seem to be intuitively aware of this distinction; the rest learn it through difficult experience. An officer's peer group widens to include older officers who hold the rank of constable and who work in the same precinct. Finally, his peer group will be comprised of all the men he works with regularly, regardless of age, years of experience, specialization or precinct.

On the job the rookie is teased, cajoled and generally given a going-over by the men. He is very unsure of himself and tries desperately to find out what is expected of him. There is the need to belong, to feel an accepted member in good standing. He takes orders from superiors; but he works day in and day out alongside those fellow officers, some of them on the force for ten or twenty years and battle-scarred veterans. What they consider to be a good policeman is very important to him. Schlossberg points out how peer group pressure can make or break a policeman:

> I have never arrested a woman for prostitution. At one precinct where I was stationed, a young woman in the neighborhood was known as the untouchable local prostitute. The cops never arrested her, for they knew she was supporting her two children by the money she earned. They felt that what she did was her business, that she was not the regular street hooker. For ten years she was ignored by the police. Then one day a young cop new to the precinct, who did not honor her special status, arrested her. She was sent to jail and her two children to institutions. The rest of the precinct was so furious at the young cop who turned her in that he had to resign from the force. They didn't like him anyhow—he was immature, headstrong, and supercilious—and the arrest was the straw that broke their tolerance. If you don't have your peers at the precinct with you, you might as well forget it. (1973:51-52)

A young officer is under very close supervision as a probationary constable. He walks the downtown beat for a year or more before he gets behind the wheel and joins a partner in the patrol car. While on the street he compares notes with his fellow rookies and tries to apply what he learned in police college. He tries hard to play the role to the satisfaction of his immediate superior, the patrol and staff sergeant, very carefully following all departmental procedures and regulations. Although he is on his own out there on the pavement, he is still in constant radio communication with headquarters and with his fellow officers on the street. He tends to be in an intensive learning situation and is usually seen but not often heard by the older officers. At any one time on the force there will not be many probationaries. In this city there has been very little new hiring in the last few years because of budget restraints. If the probationaries are to become permanent members at the end of their period of testing they have to be very careful. They are learning the practical fundamentals of police work: the forms to fill out, the procedures to follow, and the reports to be made.

Most of the problems they encounter are relatively simple; but sometimes they are called on to handle serious accidents or they are called to the scene of a fight, a holdup, or a mugging. It is with reference to these situations that estimates and evaluations are made by superior officers about his abilities and judgments. All of this goes into his file, and, since first impressions are fairly lasting, this probationary period will have a profound affect on the man's career. He may still be dropped while at police college or while he is a probationary, but this would be very exceptional. However once he becomes a fourth-class constable he joins the main stream of the police force.

While on probation the aspiring policeman makes a point of looking and acting like the other rookies. He takes his cues from them because at this time, for the most part, they are the only police he associates with, aside from his superior officers. It is in a sense like a try-out camp in football. Only the exceptional veteran bothers with the rookies, and this seldom goes beyond acknowledging their existence. It is a puzzling, lonely, insecure period for the probationaries and they group together for mutual support. At this stage most of them are young and not yet married.

Graduation to duty in patrol cars broadens the peer group and brings a new influence into the young policeman's life—he is usually with a *partner*, except on the daytime shift when he is alone. The partner will not always be the same person because of holidays, illness, overtime and other scheduling problems. As a result the new man now comes quickly into contact with men who have more years of experience than himself. Or, in a period of rapid turnover and numerous retirements, he may find that his partner has only one or two years seniority over him, and there is no generation gap. Working with the veterans, he soon encounters a variety of potential conflict situations and disagreements and quickly learns that many of the ideas he picked up at police college or as a probationary are discounted by his peer group. Unless he is very secure and independent in himself he will adapt to his new partners and operate according to their way of doing things. Obviously the first area of difficulty or conflict for him will arise when he encounters differing definitions of the police role from the different partners who belong to his newly widened peer group.

New men have to come to terms with both the prescribed and the actual manner of operations within the department. Quite often the new constable has to make a choice of trying to get along with his partner on whom he has to depend for support or to follow to the letter the rules and regulations laid down by the department. The various partners he has over the first few years can have quite divergent views about police work. The junior partner will take cues from the partners whom he admires most and whom he finds most congenial. If he happens to be saddled with a disgruntled under-achiever as a partner for any length of time he could be soured on police work. As a young policeman he will spend a lot of time after hours with the other police and will share stories and experiences. Sensitive to their reactions, he learns which approaches are approved of and which are frowned upon. He learns the general group opinions about most police matters and, at least publicly, when more experienced men are present, will accept the group wisdom with little question. After all, what does he know? He is still a rookie in his own eyes and in the eyes of his peers.

At this point in his career the young officer experiences another form of *role conflict* or difficulty. He discovers that most of his time will be spent providing small services: answering false alarms, responding to calls about noise or barking dogs, settling disputes; in short, being a peacemaker, an adviser, a conciliator and a record-keeper in the station house. This is common to most police forces across North America (Murphy, 1977). But the emphasis in his training has been on another aspect of police work, namely the law-enforcing and crime-busting role, and he tends to look upon this as the all-important aspect, the aspect that is more challenging and most approved of by his peers. Because of peer group influence he might even conceive of his role solely from this perspective and resent being sent out on calls where his abilities in human relations will be called upon. He may think that the rewards and evaluations system is heavily weighted in favor of the fearless crime buster. It takes a particularly insightful policeman to realize that keeping the peace and maintaining good community relations is, in the long run, a very effective way of controlling and solving crime. Lacking good rapport with the public and without their help the police by themselves are incapable of performing more than a holding operation as far as crime is concerned.[2] Consequently, most of the men accept the dual sub-roles of the police as important and necessary. In the practical order, although they complain about house calls involving lost cats and dogs, they realize the tremendous goodwill that this generates for the police force.

For the most part the younger policemen have rather strong and demanding views of what good police work consists of. They tend in the first five years of service to gear or shape their behavior and attitudes to these severe peer-group demands. One sergeant put it in a rather joking way:

While they're on probation they're really on their toes. Yessir, nossir. They almost make a double genuflection everytime they pass by a sergeant. As soon as they are made permanent, they change quite a bit. I suppose they really don't change that much. They hold it all in to create what they conceive to be a good impression. They know it's the sergeants they have to please because if they don't get good reports from them they don't keep the job. Once they're on permanent staff, they have the Police Association to fall back on so they are not quite as insecure. Oh, they still have to toe the line; but they learn the ropes real fast from the other guys.

Constable L. put it in a more serious way:

Young police judge each other by their willingness to lay it on the line, the frequency that they are faced with dangerous situations, even shootings and stabbings. They consider the number of difficult and dangerous cases that they successfully bring to trial. This involves the apprehension of the suspect, getting the weapons or whatever kind of evidence is required. Whenever there is a disturbance, a potential riot, a man with a gun, a holdup, they make a point of being the first rather than the last at the scene. This type of fellow when he is sent out by superior officers and ordered to clean up a house where there is a disorderly, or a potentially explosive situation at a hotel, doesn't back off. Sometimes his solution is not too subtle. Psychology doesn't seem to work too well when people are looped and when habitual troublemakers who have the reputation of intimidating everybody come at you with a broken bottle or knife. The trouble is the hard, tough, honest cop is almost at a disadvantage because he naturally makes waves and angers people both within and without the department. Although the higher-ups realize they need guys like this who are able and willing to mix it when necessary, they have to contend with a variety of people and problems and are interested in the whole operation running smoothly. There are a hell of a lot of complaints, crank calls, people to placate: the Police Commission, the public, the politicians, influential citizens, the Attorney General's office, the Police Association. I guess if the patrol police were magicians and could handle all the problems efficiently without any use of force, most people would be happy, especially the higher-ups. But that is not the way it is in the street. It's not a classroom or an office out there, it's basically a battlefield, and cowards and conscientious objectors don't win wars or even fight them.

Over the years this kind of thinking has an effect on the young men. They want to be admired, to gain status with their peers and to really belong. At the same time they also want to get ahead in the department. From this perspective they see what behavior pays off.

They notice that the careful, submissive non-critical policemen are not receiving many complaints, don't have bad reports on their records, and are even being promoted. They are caught between the demands of their peers and the demands of the system. If they are "bucking for promotion," they resolve the conflict by playing the game very carefully and strictly, according to the rules. It is not always an either/or situation but it is, without doubt, one of the most important conflicts that the policeman has to face. His choice is crucial and it will significantly affect his career pattern.

Regardless of his career plans however—whether he is satisfied to move slowly through the ranks, or quickly, or maybe even not at all—he will always be affected deeply in his thinking by the constant and close links he has with his fellow officers. The young policeman is not completely passive in this interaction; he can disagree or question or refuse to change his attitudes in any way. He may even try to change the thinking of his partners. But as he works along day-by-day there is a gradual transformation, very subtle, but real, nonetheless. Because he shares so much experience and so many situations with his partner or partners his views begin to coincide more and more with the others'. It would be very difficult for a police officer to survive on the job and not share most of the views held by his peer group.

One former policeman, speaking about this, confessed that he had felt a strong pressure to conform, to share the views of the others. He admitted that he had joined the force with an idealistic, even reformist attitude and soon found that he was odd-man-out. Rather than change his views, he decided to leave; he had found it virtually impossible to work satisfactorily with men with whom he disagreed almost constantly and rather fundamentally.[3] Many of the men indicated that they had, at times, thought of leaving but no others mentioned this particular reason for doing so. They remained, somewhat unhappy on the job, but well aware that in this period of a tight job market their options were very limited. Constable R., when asked about the fellows who had left the force answered this way:

Most of them regretted it; they never realized they had it so good. They missed the friendship, the solidarity of the men and the excitement, the membership in a virile men's organization that made them proud.

Most of the men contacted who have left the police force never mentioned the pressure to conform in their attitudes as the reason for their departure, or at least they did not feel that it was a sufficient reason to leave. There is, in fact, strong group opposition to those police who do not share, embrace wholeheartedly, and embody, the police identity. Those who represent a minority group-view can be involved in long, heated, and defensive arguments with their majority brethren. They have the choice of leaving or of remaining silent and trying to work things out unobtrusively. There is even more pressure to conform to the peer group's way of thinking when the men are organized in such a way that they are working with the same group of men regularly. In a sense each older, more experienced man with whom he comes in contact regularly becomes an informal *partial role model* for the new man if he is observant and wishes to improve his theoretical and practical approach to the job.[4] During daily patrol assignments he has a wonderful opportunity for close participant observation and he can see and compare how each experienced man handles each situation and call. The senior man is almost always in charge, except in unusual circumstances, and the newer man is back-up man wherever needed. The older man usually makes the decision and sets the tone of the encounter. Quite often one man may be more adept in handling one kind of problem as compared to others. The young man can determine for himself the extent to which he will emulate his choice of mentor or expert or role model.

Most of the policemen contacted by the author expressed the view that the man who is most respected by both his peers and his superiors is the officer who, when faced with a dangerous and very possibly explosive situation, talks to the people involved and defuses the situation, instead of resorting immediately to force which might be justified but is often counter-productive. One experienced officer described this situation:

There was a domestic recently where a young man was reported to be threatening people with an axe. If I had followed the advice of some of the younger officers who have been on special courses to learn how to deal more effectively with hostage-taking and potential violence I would have just waited him out. Instead, I took off my policeman's hat, pulled this coat up around my neck and knocked on the door. Then I went in and saw this eighteen-year-old kid with a crazy look in his eyes. He had an axe in his hand. So I said, "Hi—how are you," to him and asked him to sit down and have a cup of coffee. So we sat down and talked and, finally, the kid let go of the axe. He told me he had intended to kill his mother and brothers and sisters and was going to hang himself afterwards. He had already taken a swipe at his mother. We booked him on an assault charge and recommended psychiatric care. The judge went along with it. I hope the kid can be straightened out. I don't know what might have happened had we waited him out. Maybe nothing, or maybe, just maybe, he would have killed his mother, brothers and sisters, and himself. He had already made the noose for hanging and seemed pretty uptight. I'm glad I made the decision I did. Sure it was dangerous; but I think it could have been a real bloodbath had I waited and gone by the book. Those psychologists don't know everything. The kid knew I was a cop right away but he later told me that I seemed friendly and that it helped to cool him down. I wonder what I would have done if I had been a rookie.

It is not that this man is afraid or incapable of using force, it is just that he would much prefer to reach his objectives without resorting to force rather than make people comply with his authority and commands by physical force.

Conversely, the policeman who constantly has to prove himself by resorting to force too frequently will, in the end, defeat his own purpose. Among his fellow officers he will get the reputation of being prone to violence. Other men will begin to resent him, knowing that if they go out with him they will constantly be involved in fights and that they will be forced to support this man in questionable situations where violence could have been avoided easily by more sophisticated professional methods. Constable R recalled:

I used to have to follow this particular officer on the walking beat a few years ago. He came on strong like gang-busters all the time and, in a certain sense, created a climate of violence and resentment towards the police. I used to follow him, and because I wore blue and had a badge the people didn't distinguish. They gave me a hard time and were exceedingly cold and hateful towards me. I was reaping what he had sown. It made my shift very unpleasant and at times downright dangerous, and unnecessarily so, for the most part. I resented this officer because he made my job so much more difficult than it had to be. This guy had quite a reputation on the force and was intensely resented by the other men. He was just too quick on the draw all the time and created many problems on the force because the higher-ups were aware of the situation and had to try to keep peace among the police themselves. No, as far as I am concerned, the best kind of a policeman and the one whom most of the men admire and the young ones look up to and try to imitate, is the one who throws himself willingly, capably into the fray but only when it is really required and not before. In this case his slowness in using force stems from strength, good judgment, and professional skill, rather than weakness and cowardice. Here's another example of what I mean. The traffic cops on bikes were often pressed into service when the calls got really busy. One bitterly cold night, this traffic policeman was on patrol in the north end of the city. He was trying to stay warm, kept the motor running, but he wasn't moving much because the chill factor was really something. Well, this real character is in a squad car away at the south end of the city. He has a reputation of not answering his radio whenever he considers the calls to be uninteresting with no potential for excitement. I guess the other cars were pretty busy that night because the dispatcher couldn't get this guy in the car to respond to his call. There was a minor accident in this guy's immediate area in the south end, but he wouldn't acknowledge the call. The bike cop had to respond to the call in the south end. He nearly froze his balls off but settled things and then had to return to the north side, his regular area. The same kind of thing happened a couple of more times within an hour or so, and, by this time, the bike cop is just about frozen and really pissed-off at this other guy who isn't answering his radio and should be working his south end area. Finally, the call comes through that there is a big accident and disturbance again in the south end. So off he goes this time, anticipating at least a little excitement and change of pace. When he gets there he sees this character right there with a big crowd around, playing the hero. This fellow sees him coming and waves him off telling him that he has everything under control. The bike cop was so incensed that he just went right up to this bastard and hit him, really nailed him in front of the whole crowd. Nothing was said by anybody; but it got around pretty fast. All the guys knew about it, and they thought this guy really got what he deserved. Although the bike cop could have been in deep trouble, the whole thing was ignored higher up. I guess they all knew this guy's reputation and felt he got just what he deserved. Better than ten reprimands from them. I don't think the young fellows wanted to be much like him, although he was one really tough fellow and had quite a reputation for mixing it. You know, training with weights and really keeping in shape, the whole bit. Too damned interested in himself and screw the other guys as far as I am concerned.

Superiors as Role Models

Along with his relationship to his peers and especially his partners there is no doubt that his superior officers' reactions to him will greatly affect the policeman during his continuing socialization into the role. He is constantly being judged and evaluated by his immediate superior officers. The patrol sergeants observe his work while he is out on patrol. They are his direct support when more difficult calls have to be answered. At headquarters the staff sergeant and the inspector will examine his paperwork and his reports. Later on they will check his courtroom work and his success in making arrests that stand up in court. How well he presents his evidence in court, how well he responds to questions and cross-examination by criminal lawyers, judges, and Crown attorneys depends, first of all, on his sound judgment in the initial arrest situation, especially on the inclusion of all factors pertinent to the case in his report. The better his relationship with his superior officers, the more he sees some of them as leaders or exemplars and as possible models worthy of emulation rather than as foremen constantly checking on and even spying on the men, the more he is able to benefit and to learn from these more experienced men. Learning the job, however, is not the only thing involved here.

The patrol officer, intent on any degree of success and advancement in his professional career, realizes the importance of the evaluations made by his superiors. To the extent that he is a rational and political animal, he makes a point of discovering the feelings and views of the various sergeants with whom he must work. If he is politic he does not adopt, much less express, attitudes and behavioral tendencies and modes of operation that are at variance with those of his superiors.[5]

Superiors function as role models in two ways. If, rightly or wrongly, they are objects of real admiration and respect, they naturally cause emulation with regard to attitudes, behavior, and modes of carrying out the job and thus effect a true socialization into the identity of policeman. What they display is actually internalized. If they are seen primarily as means to success or promotion, they promote "fronting" and do not effect a real socialization; except, perhaps, insofar as the policeman now sees fronting as necessary for success and promotion and the internal effect is cynicism with respect to his own and other professions.

Conflicting Management Styles

Just as there is potential personal role-conflict for him, arising from the different ways in which the policeman's role is actually carried out by different members of his peer group, so too he encounters conflicting management styles among his superiors. This creates new stress and tension. In attempting to comply with one sergeant's or inspector's directives or requests, he may find himself at odds with another who will severely criticize him. The problem is one that is common to all complex, hierarchical organizations. But because of insistence on "the book" and on "chain of command" in police work it is more sharply evident there. For this reason inspectors and staff inspectors must confer carefully and frequently with the sergeants in order that there be as much consistency and unanimity among them as possible in their interpretation of police procedures: what rules, regulations and norms are to be enforced; which can be safely ignored or discounted.

Because he lacks an overview and because the information he has at his disposal is limited, the average policeman will be, at various times, at odds with his immediate superior over some course of action or interpretation of police procedure. Because of his rank he will be forced outwardly to comply with his superior, but not necessarily to agree with him. The more information he is given, the more rational and reasonable the sergeant's explanation of his decision is, the less conflict between the two men. However regardless of good will and effort on both sides there is always some conflict involved, for it is seldom the sergeants who are faced with the initial decision in a particular situation. The sergeants do not have to face the emotionally stressful incident itself but arrive after the fact—when things have settled down, or they simply read reports about the incident. This often affects the patrolman's decisions and puts him in a defensive position vis-a-vis the sergeant. He will attempt to justify his on-the-spot decisions and tend to resent any criticism that the sergeant levels at him. He feels that he and he alone was really in a position to assess all the factors involved in a given situation, not some sergeant who shows up after the problem has been dealt with. Inspector J. spoke one evening about his problem with sergeants:

Some of them have very little idea about dealing with men. They think they can just bark out orders, and that's all there is to it. A lot of policemen have real problems, and the sergeants should get special training in workshops and study sessions to learn about leadership, sensitivity, role definitions,[6] the proper relationship to have with the men. Many of the sergeants are very insecure. Although they may have done well out in the street themselves, this is a whole new ball game and they find it hard to change their methods and approaches. As a result they tend to ride herd on the men and give them a very tight rein. They interpret their job as being check-up specialists. Basically, it's a matter of not trusting the men and treating them like children who have to be closely supervised. I feel that the sergeants do a whole lot better job and have real rapport with the men if they look upon themselves as back-up help for the men. It's better not to intrude too much but to be available and capable of providing help of any kind. Some of the sergeants make the men look like Mickey Mouse cops especially at domestic calls. The men resent this bitterly and will sometimes go out of their way to make life pretty miserable for them.

Inspector R. adds:

I insist that the sergeants treat the men under them like men. If they show them respect, they'll get it back. I believe in discipline; but you just don't build it up on the force by spying on the men. Sure we know there are many rules being broken, smoking in the cars, going to restaurants for coffee, dogging it a bit instead of answering the radio right away. These guys just aren't machines. As long as they produce competently, I believe in giving them a fair amount of lee-way. I think they do better and want to do better. The real discipline comes from within. It is pretty hard for some of the new sergeants to understand this.

The rank-and-file policeman has some quite definite ideas about sergeants. Constable R. on the subject of Sergeant S.:

All the men really like him and think he is a fine man and a good cop. He's no patsy for anyone. They trust his judgment and obey and follow him. One of the main reasons is because he is approachable. He listens to their problems and tries to help them. The men know it will not go any further nor will it go on their record.

As a result of this the men are more responsive to Sergeant S. and obviously more receptive to his advice and point of view. They would also have the tendency to want to do a more professional job, not for his sake necessarily but, rather, because he has engendered in them a certain amount of pride and confidence.

By way of contrast, Constable L. was feeling a bit discouraged one day and complained:

Everything goes on your record and is held against you. Even if you are cleared, it still appears, so I'm pretty fearful of complaints laid against me. The judg-ment and punishment is meted out by a kangaroo court of my superiors. Hell, I'm better off if a case goes to a civil court. At least there I have the benefit of legal aid and defence. As far as these damn sergeants and inspectors are con-cerned I don't even have the same rights as the lowest citizen.

The sergeants themselves see their work and responsibility from a variety of angles. Sergeant L. had just been promoted recently and was still obvi-ously inexperienced and insecure in his new role:

I keep a close check on my men not only to keep the pressure on the slackers but also especially so that I can be in a position to make a knowledgeable and honest evaluation of the men. I am not being very responsible or fair if I merely shoot the shit with other sergeants about a guy I know next to nothing about.

One night while on patrol with Sergeant V., this same man said:

A good patrol sergeant has quite a responsibility in the field. He should be there on the spot, if anything very serious happens, for consultation, direction, and advice. I see myself mainly as a teacher, not in the classroom sense but right out there where all the action is.

Very soon after, and as though in illustration of his meaning, the car was called to the scene of a cold, wet, intoxicated fourteen-year-old girl lying in a ditch. A squad car was there already but it was the sergeant who made the decisions and called for an ambulance. Nevertheless, the case still remained the responsibility of the constables and they wrote up the report. It was difficult to tell from their demeanor whether they resented or appreciated the presence of the sergeant.

At another time Sergeant F., one of the old-timers, volunteered this opinion of his younger colleagues:

The trend today among the younger police is to be not so willing to risk injury. In my day we had to use muscle quite a bit. These fellows tend to be more dependent on a gun. They try to avoid too much involvement in order to protect their job. They are very security-conscious, which is very understandable. They do not want to be fired if they get badly injured on the job.

Sergeant O., relatively new, spoke in a similar manner:

I'm very critical and hard on hotshot policemen who don't follow the rules. I believe in checking on my men, supporting them, so that I can be in a position to make proper evaluation and judgment of their abilities and performance. I think the rules, regulations and norms are there for a purpose. They sort of create uniformity and teamwork. I don't like the grumbling of individualistic policemen who by-pass the rules and want to run their own show. They usually create a lot of problems for both themselves and everybody else. I really don't understand the reason for this. It would be so much easier and effective the other way. Of course, in the olden days, the younger policemen were with the more experienced men for a much longer period of time and after a while began to understand the rationale behind some of the rules. As a result they didn't go off hot-headed and make a lot of serious and stupid mistakes. Nowadays, with the larger number coming in at any one time, the young hotshots tend to go out all together, disregarding orders and not answer their radios too well. If they would only slow down a bit and learn their job well, they would come to an awareness and understand why these rules were made and why they should be kept.

On the other hand, the younger the men were, the more they expressed the feeling that the whole system of rules, regulations, and procedures needed revamping. Constable C. had this to say:

A lot of the rules are pointless except to make our life more miserable. We are being forced to work under 1920 rules in a whole new ballgame. The criminals are using new tricks, so we damn well better get with it. Some of those senior officers who insist on some of these chicken-shit rules are out of touch with the street. A lot of things have changed out there. It's not the same kind of ball-game. Hell, it's not even the same ballpark sometimes. What worked in the old days doesn't necessarily work now; so let's get rid of those regulations that are useless and cancel them right off the books. Try telling that to those old war horses upstairs and see what happens. They're still hung up on hair-length and style for Chrissake.

This was not happening because "the brass" were fearful of change that might diminish their authority or provide evidence that their thinking might be outmoded. The young men felt that they were already at a tremendous disadvantage and wanted the odds a little more equal. Because of their greater experience, the older the men were, the less they were in disagreement with the superiors and, consequently, the less conflict they had to resolve in their own minds. This is a good example of generation gap. There can be a form of differential treatment and even of harassment by superior officers who are not overly interested in aiding, abetting, or supporting those younger police whose opinions are considered not necessarily treacherous, but definitely subversive and insidious, especially with respect to group solidarity.

The social control mechanism is operated by the majority group members through mockery, harassment, and bickering. There are also superiors who might resort to giving labelled troublemakers dirtier and more difficult jobs and hours and, at the end of all this, poor evaluations as well. The pressure is on the new policeman to "shape up" and think "white and right." If a person's ideas are deemed "too far out" he is forced eventually to resign or to reject his deviant ways. To be drummed out of the corps is a fearful punishment for men who thrive on group support and in-group solidarity, and who are ill-prepared for another calling.

Television

Our city is a border city receiving the television programming of both the American and Canadian networks. In any week there are at least six police-related programs available to its citizens. They are an additional source of role models for the budding police officer. Since, in a sense, today's rookie is a product of the television era in which police programs became popular, he may have built up in his own mind a distorted image of what real police work is like. To the degree that he was, and continues to be, affected by these unreal, glamorized television versions of role models, to that degree he may mistakenly try to imitate them. The real world and the world of television can become intertwined and confused if he has spent a good part of his youth being influenced and having his perceptions shaped by hours of television viewing. Some inspectors spoke of "culture shock" suffered on the part of the new recruits when they rejoined the real world out on patrol. For some there is a real problem "re-entry" from the fantasized consciousness formed by television to consciousness of the plain everyday world of reality on the beat. If a sufficient number of young rookies are assigned to one precinct or one division this creates an interesting and potentially troublesome situation. All these men sharing the same idealized television role models of police and reinforcing each other in this respect could, and sometimes do, try to emulate these role models and to carry out their duties in ways that are quite contrary to the department's directives. Sergeants confronted with this new breed have an additional problem to cope with, namely, a whole age group of young police who attempt to live out in real life the glamorized fantasy-land of the television police-hero. Many sergeants complained that the influence of television police stories accounted for some of the younger men's difficult behavior and attitudes.

Summary

In this chapter we have seen the structure of the police force, the early training, the promotion system, and the rules and regulations as formative factors in the occupational socialization of the policeman. His mode of perceiving and reacting to these forces determines the degree of influence they have on him. We have also seen the expectations, sometimes conflicting, laid on him by peers, partners, superiors, and ghosts on television to adapt, to imitate and to identify.

In the following chapter we will look at what the public and the police expect from each other. The police deal constantly with the public; how they perceive and define each other will determine significantly the character of their encounters. How an actor performs depends to a certain extent on the type of audience he faces and on the response he anticipates.

Notes

1. For a discussion of reference group see Shibutani, 1955.
2. See Murphy, 1977.
3. This is an example of selective attrition wherein a policeman whose views are so incompatible with organizational demands and peer group wisdom that he resigns.
4. The term *role model* refers here to the more experienced officers whom the younger officers can choose to emulate. The role model can be one or many, and he may have a positive or negative effect on the young officer. He is generally from the officer's same rank but could in some instances be an admired or capable superior officer. The young officer may decide to emulate

56

the role model only in a limited, partial way, picking and choosing that aspect or quality of the role model that he feels he is capable of imitating or that he considers worthy of imitation or emulation.

5. There is an important difference between *dedicated imitation* for whatever purposes and what Goffman labels as a *front*, i.e. "that part of the individual's performance which regularly functions in a general and fixed fashion to define the situation for those who observe the performance" (1959: 22-30).

6. The reader will understand that the inspector being quoted has had some contact with sociology (Ed.)

Chapter 4

The Policeman and His Public

People are influenced by and respond to the expectations of others. Policemen are especially influenced by and tend to react to what they consider to be public expectations.[1] This chapter will explore some of the reasons why these expectations have a negative effect on the police and how these tend to isolate the police from other members of society.

Reciprocal Expectations

According to Homans, people's behavior is based on the principle of pain vs. pleasure; that is to say, people tend to seek those things which are pleasurable and to avoid those which cause pain. The public tends, in its contacts with the police, to expect these encounters to be, for the most part, unpleasant. To receive a stern warning or a traffic citation are not regarded as pleasant experiences. The policeman carries a gun and a night-stick and has been known to use them. Consequently, most of one's encounters with the police are regarded, or are expected to be, negative. Resentment and hostility towards police may result and may form the basis of each contact of the public with the police.[2].

Rather than expecting positive, personally fulfilling encounters, the policeman often comes to expect violent or abusive responses from the public. So, in a sense, both the police and the public tend to view their direct contacts with one another negatively. For the policeman, sometimes, there are rewarding patterns of interaction that make working in an often unbearable environment seem worthwhile. According to most policemen these rewarding experiences with the public are infrequent:

We are all alone out there. Nobody, but nobody will come to help us but a fellow-policeman if we get into trouble. We depend on each other very much. Everybody else is an outsider; you can't really count on them when you've got your back up against a wall. The public want to have their cake and eat it. They want lots of law and order, to be able to walk on the streets safely; but just

*watch all the crying if we resort to strong-arm tactics or curbside justice—we're
in trouble, and the public gets all upset. You're damned if you do and damned if
you don't. The safest thing for us to do is keep our nose clean and to ignore a
lot. It means less hassle for us; but I think it means that more violence and trouble occurs. But, if that is the way the public wants it, then they shouldn't cry if
things gradually get out of hand.*

We are not speaking of just one day or of a few days, but of almost every
working day, and, not infrequently, of days when the policemen are off
duty. Individuals often obtain their ego support from their audience, that is,
from people with whom they interact. Who makes up the audience the
policeman plays to? He tries to maintain a subdued professional image, and
certainly the uniform and the mystique of police work is important to his
self-concept. However when very frequently confronted with a hostile, or
non-supportive audience, or with the anticipation of such an audience, what
can the policeman do to maintain a positive self-image?

Actors who are in a badly reviewed play often have to rely upon the positive criticism and support of their fellow actors. The policeman, because of
the very nature of his work, expects that his audience, generally, will be
critical.[3] As a result of experience in the field, the policeman gradually
becomes less interested in what the public thinks of his performance and
more about how his fellow policemen evaluate his work. This is the normal
reaction of anyone who perceives himself as a member of a beleaguered and
despised minority group.[4]

Every day policemen face individuals who belong to different social
classes, to different racial, ethnic, religious, and occupational groups. As the
police fulfil their responsibilities toward individual members of their public
human interactions take place and relationships are developed; these may
last for seconds or for a very long time; they may be very intense or they
may be superficial. The people involved all form part of the officer's occupational role-set or public, and they respond to him, not as a civilian, not as
a whole person, but in his capacity as policeman. The policeman has to
learn, sometimes in a hard way, what public expectations are and how to
live with the conflict and the stress that arise from the different role expectations of his public. He cannot always depend on consistent reactions from
the different members of his public. He cannot even depend on consistent
patterns of action from the same person whom he contacts at different times
and under different circumstances. Unlike clergy, doctors, lawyers, social
workers and members of other helping professions who can count on a certain degree of acceptance and shared role expectations, the policeman cannot always anticipate positive and grateful responses. If he does step out of
his expected role for a moment, he does so at risk. His life, or health, or reputation might be placed in serious jeopardy.

Also, unlike those in the service occupations, the policeman on patrol has very little control over his working environment or his audience. He does not choose the time, the place, the type of encounter nor the individuals to whom he must respond. This fundamental lack of control creates a certain amount of frustration in him. Unlike doctors or lawyers, his clients are not screened by a nurse or receptionist who makes an appointment for that client. He goes wherever he is sent by the dispatcher who picks the patrol car that is closest and available. He must deal with the unexpected and the bizarre. He is called in to help when people are often emotionally upset, excited, nervous, angry and fearful and when he himself may be very tired and struggling with his own problems. If he is carrying out his duties adequately he cannot avoid, postpone or competently make an appointment for another day or a more convenient hour.

Coping with the Public

In order to deal with the unexpected and the diverse in his audience the policeman over the years develops coping mechanisms to minimize some of the stressful conditions of his work. He will attempt to be always on the alert, to notice patterns and similarities. He tends to form his own highly personal opinions about the various groups with whom he comes in contact on the job. They include criminals of various kinds, law-abiding citizens, and members of different ethnic occupational and social groups, politicians, bikers and upstanding citizens. Each one of these groups or subcultures in its turn has its own view, often stereotypical, about the police and their functions. Bikers, for instance, a relatively new subcultural group, have very definite, negative views about the police. According to several who were interviewed, the police were licensed thugs and sadists who unjustly harass bikers and who attempt to make life as miserable as possible for them. The police, in their turn, do not hold the bikers to be acceptable role models for youth. As one can see, the police and the bikers have very definite ideas as to what to expect from each other and, whenever bikers were stopped while on patrol, there was always mutual hostility that was evident just below the surface. In a sense, each contact had a prescribed scenario similar to a boxing match with the police and bikers shifting and sparring, replaying several previous episodes. The individual actors may not have been the same each time, but the pattern of the encounter held few surprises. A young, inexperienced policeman or biker could upset the entire play by initiating an unfamiliar action or response. The rigid, stereotypical format of the encounters tends, of course, to limit any understanding or dialogue between the two groups. The pattern of the relationship is set and serious consequences could befall anyone who fails to act out the role in the manner prescribed.

He will lose support within his own group and his credibility will be brought into question.

The police are well prepared for this type of situation with those they consider to be predictable actors such as bikers or criminal lawyers whose role behavior is well defined and understood—at least to the satisfaction of the police. In a sense, the police feel comfortable with these groups because they feel that they know what to expect and are prepared for it. However, when they are faced with individuals about whom they know very little they feel themselves placed at a disadvantage. They do not know what to expect and, because of this, they become more wary and suspicious. In order to minimize this uncertainty, and to cope with it, the police sharpen their powers of observation. This is done with the intention of categorizing people into groups, thereby making their behavior not only more understandable but more predictable as well. Since police work is carried out frequently under unusual and stressful conditions it is very important for them to do this as a means of reducing the unexpected, and therefore potentially dangerous, aspects of their work. It is a form of shorthand that they believe helps them make decisions more quickly and accurately. The categories and attitudes about the people in those categories are not always based on objective fact; nor are they always empathetic. Rather they are an amalgam of the policeman's own experiences strengthened and reinforced by general police folklore. A more detailed presentation of these attitudes and stereotypes about the various members of the policeman's public is given in Chapter 7.

As a means of personal survival the policeman concerns himself, primarily, with the opinions and expectations of his peers. It is conceivable he might feel that most of the public are contemptuous in their attitudes toward the police. If he is equally convinced that his peers and superiors do not have a very high opinion of him either then his position becomes almost untenable and he will find himself a very lonely and isolated individual. It is for his own survival and well-being that the policeman increasingly avoids unnecessary contact with the public who, he believes, are never really satisfied. Their demands and definitions of his role are so often, in his opinion, unreasonable and contrary to reality. He prefers the company and support of the men with whom he feels at home and at ease. No fronts, no games, are necessary. He can finally relax with those who know and understand him because they too share the burden and the demands of the role.

Summary

In this chapter, we have seen how images of expected and predictable behavior determine the manner in which the public and the police regard each other. These stereotypical attitudes often make it difficult for the police and the public to react positively in their encounters with one another. They have the effect of creating needless additional stress for them. The following chapter will take up this theme of stress in the policeman's work relating to two areas of the policeman's contact with his public: in the streets and in the courtroom. Again, the policeman will speak for himself pointing out principally that stress can be not only debilitating in its effects but also a very powerful factor in the process of socialization into the policeman's role.

Notes

1. In general, the majority of the Canadian public express satisfaction with police services; their respect for police is increasing. They do *not* consider the police too powerful, or overpaid, or dishonest and unfair in their treatment of citizens. This finding is contrary to the local police-view about the public they serve. (Poll in *Weekend Magazine*; Toronto, August 26, 1978; p. 3.)
2. For an excellent study of the police and the public see Reiss, 1971.
3. It is worthwhile recalling the fact that, aside from the military, the police are the only group in society who have the legal right to employ force in carrying out their duties.
4. See Goldstein (1971: 306-318) for further insights on this theme.

PART III

Interacting with the Environment

Chapter 5

The Impact of Stress Situations

The Nature of Stress

There is a certain amount of stress that is inherent in every occupation as, indeed, there is in most aspects of daily life. According to Selye (1974: 26-32) stress is the non-specific response of the body to any demand made upon it. Whether or not the agent or situation that is producing stress is pleasant or unpleasant is immaterial. He uses the term *stressor* to mean any event or situation that causes stress. What ensues is a non-specific demand to readjust oneself to a new situation or agent. Selye further maintains that only excessive stress needs to be avoided or reduced, and he prefers the term *distress* to describe this situation. Distress can be the result of deprivation of stimuli as well as of excessive stimulation. In either case the person's ability to cope with distress is severely taxed and produces negative effects on him which he calls *strain*. The effect of the stress can be long-lasting even after the stressor has ceased to act. Stress in his view can be both helpful as well as harmful, depending on the person and on the circumstances.

Applying stress theory to the occupational situation, Kroes (1976: 4-8) defines *job stress* as occupational pressures which adversely affect workers and *job stressors* as individual negative factors which produce that stress.

The negative effects of stressors are called *job strains*, and they lead to reduced efficiency at work, personality change, health problems, and harmful coping mechanisms.

Coping with Stress

What can the police do that would enable them to handle bad stress or distress better and minimize the strain on them? Kroes (1976: 108-118) suggests that the police be trained in stress-awareness and understanding, and be armed with a basic knowledge of human behavior. Policemen should also be taught how to act and deal with specific stressful job situations such as family crises and racial conflict.

He points out that, for some people, stress is necessary as a motivator. Thus the stress in some occupations provides a challenge that allows a person to utilize a multitude of his abilities and that also satisfies his needs for achievement, activity, creativity, importance, personal growth, development, and recognition. The policeman's occupation is certainly challenging enough, and challenge is one of the main reasons cited by the police for joining the force.

The crisis situations that he encounters in the line of duty are a normal and inescapable part of his occupation. How the policeman deals with them can determine to a great extent his success or failure as a policeman. It is the contention of this researcher that the average policeman, especially in larger cities, is faced with a wider variety and a greater number of potential sources of stress than most other occupations and that he is affected in varying degrees by all of them.[1] How he is modified by previous stressors will determine to a certain extent how the police officer deals with each new stressful crisis situation. There is an interplay operating here at all times. If he handles the situations "well" this means that his peers and superiors are as satisfied with his performance as he is himself. This successful, or approved, carrying out of his duties will lessen the impact and strain on him of the stressful encounters. If, however, he handles the stress situation "poorly" either in his own eyes or those of his peers or superiors, this intensifies the role strain. It makes the policeman increasingly subject to the debilitating long-range effects of cumulative role strain.

Unless he learns in the harshest school of all, the dangerous arena of the street, what to do and what not to do the next time, unless he profits from his mistakes and gets some feedback and constructive criticism from peers and superiors, he will tend to repeat the same mistakes and create additional problems for himself and the department. He is well aware that every case and incident that he is confronted with is different and requires special treatment. He is constantly admonished never to treat any situation as routine or in an offhanded manner. This is survival wisdom. If he profits from his mistakes and successes he will feel some intrinsic satisfaction on the job; he will become more self-assured and gradually will cope better with trying, stressful situations, calling on a backlog of experiences in which his interventions and methods of operation were successful. As a result of this growth in professional expertise and personal confidence a policeman will have less need to seek various negative coping mechanisms that never fully satisfy or compensate for his failure in satisfactorily carrying out his major role obligations.[2]

The actual encounters involving a high degree of stress are the most important single factor in the socialization into the role. The effect of these experiences on the person is more lasting and fundamental because they are intense and, furthermore, it is in the light of his performance in these situations that the policeman is judged and judges himself. It is not just the impact of the incident itself that is being spoken of here but rather the entire situation, involving the feedback from his peers, his superiors, the courts and the public, that becomes the main learning dynamic.

Stress for the policeman, however, is further specified by another important factor. There are occupations where the stress is situational such as emergency-ward personnel or air-traffic controllers where the individual is under almost constant stress while he is on the job. The police on the other hand experience long periods of relative relaxation and even boredom coupled with periods of high-stress encounters with the public. It is during and after these stressful situations that the policeman, because of heightened awareness and emotional strain, learns the most about his occupation. His right to resort to *the legitimate use of force and the law* is a constant backdrop or factor that makes the policeman's role different from all other occupations. The possible use of force or the law on his part is always present whenever he is involved in a stressful encounter with the public. This ever-present possibility or potential for force and violence heightens the stress inherent in the encounter and, thus, also intensifies the learning process.

Whether or not a person is going to become a capable policeman is ultimately determined in the street. It is the harsh school of experience that teaches him. If he cannot profit from mistakes, if the role stress is too much, if he doesn't learn to use "good judgment," he will fail as a policeman, in his own eyes and those of his peers and superiors.

To the degree that he perceives in himself incompetence and lack of growth and development on the job, to the extent that he finds little satisfaction in his efforts, he will react in a variety of ways. In years past when the job was low-paying he might have handed in his resignation and gone to some other occupation less demanding and, perhaps, better paying. Nowadays with good salary, good pension plans, and jobs scarce, this option is not always open. The man may therefore remain on the force as a minimal performer and resort to a variety of coping mechanisms in order to survive.

He may decide to avoid as many trying situations as possible and thus avoid making mistakes. He might try to cover up his inabilities by playing politics, in the hope that this will strengthen his position when time for promotion comes around. He may, and this is the most common reaction, simply go through the motions, stay out of trouble, and try to hang on until retirement age. Quite often these attempts to handle problems on the job are accompanied by a variety of coping behaviors off the job: alcoholism, absenteeism, malingering, and promiscuity. There is an element of self-defeat and self-hatred involved here and, regardless of the position on the force that he manages to reach, if the policeman sees himself as an incompetent failure he will often try to cover it up and become either a loud, sarcastic, possibly brutal policeman on the job, or else he may turn inward and become a loner, a recluse, painfully and sadly playing out the string.

At School in the Streets

The most important factor shaping the values, attitudes and behavior patterns of the policeman are the crisis situations which he confronts and the impact that they have on him.[3] When the police were asked for the most important factor affecting and shaping their lives they cited, almost to a man, actual high-stress incidents on patrol in which they had been involved and from which they felt they had learned the most. One officer put it this way:

Sure I feel stress—from the time I put on the uniform till I've finished my eight hours. I never know when I'm going to have to resort to force or make arrests; but the possibility is always there. I have to learn to live with it. It's no big deal. It's part of the job. I don't feel guilty after I've been in some dirty mess out on the street—as long as I've done my best. I'm always a bit worried about how I'll handle it. Too much force and I'm maybe up on a complaint. Not enough, and the guy gets away or makes a fool out of me. I've learned how to handle myself out there especially in pressure situations. Sure I've made mistakes; but I think I've learned from them. My bosses see to that when they review my work. Maybe you can hide your mistakes, professor, but it's a little tougher for us to hide ours because we work out there, and we're observed by a lotta people. There is never any shortage of grandstand quarterbacks to second-guess us. But it's me who is laying it on the line out there every day—not them. I'm a bit scared; that's healthy and normal; it's more a matter of being nervous. I want to call a good game and maybe make a few big plays. It's a challenge. I guess that's what I like about it most. No humdrum nine-to-five desk job for me.

Many mentioned how they had made mistakes because they just did not know what to do. They were under stress and tension; they were ill-prepared for the problems; they did the best they could. After the incident they had time to think, to discuss, to ponder, and to evaluate along with their peers and superiors what they could learn and how they should change in order to be better prepared for similar situations. Despite police and college training and a period of probation during which they are closely observed, the police do not feel they are adequately trained or prepared to confront the wide range of human problems with which they now have to deal almost every day. Constable R. stated:

I don't think we are really effective policemen until we have been on the force for at least ten years. As a young cop, I was poorly prepared to cope with the problems of my new role. The failure and problems that I personally experienced as a patrol officer shaped and formed me into what I am today.

The policemen cited, with ease, incidents from their own personal experience which, they felt, had left an impression on them and from which they had learned to be, in their own eyes, better policemen. Constable L. had this to say:

There is not much question that most effective learning processes would be from actual road work. This does not always include a dangerous crisis. I want to give you some details about a situation that happened about three years ago which I feel opened up my eyes to things that I had read about but never personally experienced. I had been on the police force for approximately two years, only six months of this time was in car patrols. Along with two other officers I was dispatched by radio to a core-city home early in the morning concerning a shooting. On arrival I observed a man, forty-five to fifty years old, lying in a bed with a gunshot wound to his head. Running around the home were eight to ten children, all under thirteen years of age. Upon checking the home I found two female dogs both of which had litters around them. The house wasn't fit for a pig—no pun intended. The home was full of dirt, old clothing, one bed for the father. The bath was half-full of old stale water and flies too numerous to even guess at the amount. The children all slept in two rooms with dogs as roommates and mattresses and old clothing for beds. It was under these circumstances that I feel I learned more in three short hours than my two previous whole years. Upon investigation of the shooting we found that the man had attempted suicide. After he was removed to the hospital, we started to attempt to care for and help the children who knew of no other way of life. I contacted friends of the family, relatives and neighbors and they cared for all the children. The Children's Aid and the Humane Society were also contacted. A complete report of all our findings and observations were submitted, including our feelings about it. After a very short time all children were relocated and the house was subsequently condemned. It is in the above case that I realized the need for and work which social agencies can do, when properly notified. I further learned that the lower classes, in cases such as this, can't be helped unless someone puts a hand out to help them.

This particular policeman remembered this incident very vividly and was obviously affected by the extreme poverty and misery that he encountered.

He knew from his own eyes, ears, nose and hands what some people were up against and why social agencies are necessary. This episode seems to have made this particular policeman a little more reluctant to make snap judgments and more inclined to take into account family background and environmental factors when dealing with juvenile delinquents.

Crisis situations that the police have to handle often create wide repercussions if they are dealt with incorrectly. The policeman is admonished to proceed carefully and prudently, not to jump to conclusions and to be observant. It seems to take several cases similar to the ones about to be described for this lesson to be learned. Constable R. described two crisis situations:

I attended a bad accident scene where I observed a man trapped in a car. I could feel no pulse and felt that the man was dead. The ambulance drivers arrived, examined the man and were also convinced that he was dead. With the aid of cutting tools we freed the body and, on checking the man again, I wasn't so sure, so I ordered the ambulance men to take him to the nearest hospital. When he arrived at the hospital he was placed on machinery that could keep his heart beating. As far as the attending physician was concerned, he was technically alive. Three hours later the man did die. Back at the scene I was asked by a friend of the deceased man what his condition was, and I almost replied that the man was dead, but I caught myself and answered that he appeared critical to me. With that, the friend left and returned with the deceased's family to the hospital. I cannot imagine the shock to a family member if he is told that his relative is dead and then arrives at the hospital to hear that he is alive.

It is difficult to be alert and sensitive enough to not only do the proper things but also to say the proper thing while under pressure. A professional person can do this and still be kind and thoughtful without getting emotionally involved. There are seldom any blueprints for the proper course of action. If the policeman follows the prescribed rules and procedures he can be technically correct, but if he overlooks the human element he can hurt people when they are most disturbed. The following incident vividly points out how appearances can be very deceiving and how, if precipitous action is taken, it can create serious problems. Constable R.:

In a suicide case a father went out into his backyard twenty feet [6 metres] from the closed back door of his house, placed a twelve-gauge shotgun in his mouth, and pulled the trigger. We didn't know this when a neighbor spotted the body and phoned the police. When we arrived we found that the body was cold. As it turned out, it had been there for about two hours before our arrival. On checking the house, I found all doors and windows closed with storm windows and doors. Through a front window I could see another body on a chesterfield, partially clothed, female. Through another window I could see a youth sitting at a table, about twenty years old, [sic] with a box of shotgun shells on a refrigerator beside him. Considering that it might be a double murder, a suicide and murder, or just suicide, we entered front and back at the home at the same time and took hold of the twenty-year-old. I learned, surprisingly, the truth about the incident. Apparently the family did not hear the shot only twenty feet [6 metres] away, but outside. The mother, the wife of the deceased, was sound asleep on the chesterfield. I had to do a complete turn around in my thinking and began assisting this family that only a few minutes earlier I thought was possibly involved in a murder.

Had the policemen acted on their first impulses and gone into the house with guns drawn, expecting the youth to react, they might have created serious trouble. They learned in a very tragic situation that things are often not what they appear to be and to proceed carefully, despite appearances; proper procedures can help them to avoid serious mistakes.

Constable L. mentioned this situation in which he was involved:

Once, while I was on motorcycle patrol I had occasion to be involved in a large-scale riot. You remember the one. There was a hell of a lot of trouble. It all started with about one hundred youths who had gathered at the P—— grounds and were causing damage. Just as the shows were closing for the night and more youths were on their way home, the radio stations let out the riot news. They were sure a great help. Before we knew it, there were about a thousand young people milling around and getting ugly. Pretty soon they swarmed into the downtown streets and caused a lot of damage. What struck me at the time were the many youths who I knew personally to be law-abiding citizens. They were caught up in this uncontrolled riot, although many of them were really only curious spectators. One youth approached me later that week after things had quieted down and stated that he had not even wanted to be there. He was carried along by his buddies who were itching for a little excitement. At the time of the riot I had felt badly because persons whom I counted on seemed to be lined up with the group against me. You know, there were a lot of policemen injured in that mess, especially those who got there first. I learned from that encounter that I would never judge a situation or people until I knew all the facts fully.

In this instance, the policeman is actually fighting for his life and apparently sees some of his friends join in the fight against the police. He could have, on the basis of the immediate evidence, become very disillusioned with his so-called friends and could have jumped to the conclusion that all the young people were troublemakers, including his former friends. Under the circumstances this would be the logical conclusion, but things are not always what they appear to be.

Constable G. had this to say:

It has been my policy as a policeman to treat everyone the same and I have practised this rule all through my career. It has got me into trouble, sometimes, with the higher-ups but I can still live with myself. The guys have given me the nickname "Fairshake" and I am happy about that.

I once was asked to work with a young officer who had the capability of becoming a good police officer. After working with him for about a month and having him stand by and listen to my way of approaching a situation, I gave him his first opportunity to approach a woman whom we had stopped for a traffic offence. This young officer was brash, sometimes arrogant, quick-witted, fairly well-educated, fearless in any situation and somewhat handsome. He had a lot going for him. He approached the car, cockily pushing his cap back on his head, and demanded in a loud voice the necessary identification papers without telling her what the offence was! Within a minute he had her crying, then angry, then she came out of her car swinging her purse. The scene was deteriorating very quickly and so when I interfered the young officer was about to arrest her for assault. After apologizing to the woman and calming her down, I explained the offence to her, issued her a summons and allowed her to proceed.

I don't think the young officer was very happy but I felt that I had to step in because he was not handling the situation very well. From then on I made up my mind that everytime I stopped a person I would think back on this incident and act exactly in the opposite manner of the young officer. Although I had failed with him, I personally learned a lesson which has stayed with me for many years. I guess you might say I learned a reverse lesson by observing the negative results when one proceeds in a very unprofessional and foolish manner while carrying out one's responsibilities. I think a lot of policemen create their own problems by proceeding in an incompetent and aggravating way. It has been my experience that the majority of citizens respond well if they are treated politely and professionally. This young officer is still having problems today because he is so awkward in his human relations.

Constable G. is no longer a young man; but he continues to learn from situations he encounters on the job. In this case he learned how he should not proceed. From what he said it appears that his partner was vividly demonstrating exactly how one should not proceed as a policeman. In a sense this episode was an unrehearsed refresher course for the senior policeman who learned again a lesson that instructors tried to teach him a long time ago. His younger partner, apparently less receptive, didn't learn the lesson and continues to create his own little hell on the job while cursing the public and criticizing his peers.

Constable L. cites this example:

In November 1972 at about 11:15 a.m., a routine bank-alarm call was broad-

*cast and two units responded to the bank at —— and —— Roads. Upon the
arrival of the first car, it was learned that the alarm was turned in as a result of
an armed holdup and a radio broadcast was issued concerning a wanted car and
its two male occupants. Shortly after 11:20 a.m., the wanted car was observed
in the South —— area, and car X took chase. The wanted car at first simply
fled the police as would be expected, and the wild chase was on. After several
blocks the wanted car slowed down to nearly a stop and waited for car X to
catch up to them. Then the robbers opened up with rifles and sawed-off shotguns
on the police and very narrowly missed the officers in the cruiser. They were
later cornered, arrested, and convicted. I use this example because I think that
I, as well as too many policemen, reign supreme in this type of situation. It was
only through luck and not experience that the two officers in pursuit were not
seriously injured or killed because this type of robbery and high-speed chase
happens rarely in our city. I do feel that it wiped a high and mighty attitude
from the personality of a number of officers. Certainly those two men in car X
realize how close they came to cashing in their chips. I think they will proceed
with more caution in the future. A .38 revolver is no match for a rifle or a .357
magnum.*

Constable L. was in one of the cars that was involved in cornering the robbers and saw, on the spot, the distress of the two officers who had been
involved in the shooting. They would relive this episode frequently in their
imaginations and no amount of talking or explaining would be as effective
as this experience in moving them to become more cautious and prudent.

Constable M. related this incident:

*Back in 1965 when I had only been on the job about a year I was working alone
in a small suburban police department. I was sent to a family dispute involving
a woman who was experiencing some mental or emotional strain and had
locked herself in her house with her four-year-old child. I was able to get into
the house where I found her huddled in the kitchen holding her child in one arm
and a large butcher-knife in the other. She kept saying she was going to kill the
child and then herself. I was successful in talking her into giving up the knife
and allowing the child to go free. From this I learned never to go into a situation like this alone unless it is absolutely necessary and also that compassion for
a person in a situation such as this sometimes is all that is needed to resolve the
matter.*

This particular episode was successfully resolved, but without a back-up
man or partner at *domestics* a policeman can be in a very dangerous or compromising situation. Policemen in general do not like responding to domestics because they are so potentially explosive and emotionally draining.
Furthermore, if a woman is involved and the policeman is alone she can

easily lay a complaint against him, and he can find himself in a very difficult position. Alone, he has no police witness to corroborate his statements and explanations.

Constable V. recalled a domestic of his:

My first major learning experience was in the line of a domestic-type call. I, unfortunately, took the side of a beaten wife who was obviously unable to defend herself against her husband. None too gently, I arrested the husband and later in court I found myself being accused of various wrongdoings, not only by the husband but also by the wife to whom I had lent my support. It was a bitter lesson for me to learn that it is a wise officer who listens to both sides of a dispute and never commits himself to lending support to either party.

No matter how often the policeman is warned to remain neutral on domestic calls, it seems he has to be burned once or twice before the well-meant advice is internalized. According to the police, the woman in a family squabble feels that she is at the mercy of her husband since she knows he can beat her again. If she lays charges against him she could lose her only means of support and, when she calms down, this factor looms large in her decisions. The policeman learns that he can do very little at domestics except to calm the people down, give both parties some advice and refer them to the social agencies that are in a position to help them.

Constable W. had this to say:

Police officers are great talkers. The main topic of conversation usually involves the various calls answered by others and how they dealt with them. I can recall being very critical of a brother officer when I learned that, in the pursuit of another car, he had "lost" it due to the fact that he had not attained great speeds and had been unwilling to risk running red lights. My own chance came soon enough and, showing great courage and daring, I romped after a car, running red lights and travelling just as fast as I could. It wasn't until my senior partner reached over and shut off the ignition that I actually had a chance to collect my thoughts and smarten up a bit. In retrospect, I know now that my driving was not only dangerous but was in a certain sense a form of cowardice on my part. I could have totalled the car and injured or killed people, ploughing through a red light. At the time, I felt that to lose a car I was pursuing would be a defeat for me, and I was afraid that I might be criticized in the same manner that I had criticized my partner.

As a result of the older man's actions this officer came to understand himself better. Speeding through red lights is very exciting on television but in real life the policeman does this at his own risk and is in serious trouble if he has an accident. Generally, when this was pointed out, the man slowed down and checked both approaches before proceeding through a red light.

The officer felt now that he had been arrogant and overly critical of his fellow officers. From now on, the car would be kept under control. What had been seen earlier as cowardice or, at least, as reluctance to take any chances in the carrying out of one's duties, is now understood as prudent police action which, in the long run, is more effective.

Constable C. gave this report:

A valuable learning experience for me was when a close friend of mine was promoted to sergeant. I was sure that this was my "in" with the department and would raise my status in the eyes of others. On a particular call, the new sergeant gave me very precise and explicit instructions which were contrary to my own thoughts and ways of doing things. I chose to adopt my own methods. As things often will, everything went sour for me on the call but I wasn't worried because after all I had my friend the sergeant! Much to my surprise the sergeant gave me a severe tongue-lashing and was seriously considering having me charged under the Police Act. My feelings of hostility and resentment only began to ease when it dawned on me that he was really a fine man who had disregarded a friendship to ensure that I didn't go wrong. When working with him now, he is my sergeant—period. He is a friend only when the shift is over.

This episode is a good example of the difficulties involved in conflicting role relationships. The officer learned that, on the job, friendship gives way to strict rank relationships within a hierarchical structure. In other words, primary relationships give way to secondary ones in most official business. This particular police officer now understood from hard experience that there are certain job requirements that should be adhered to, and that, if one takes advantage of a friendship in order to disregard a legitimate command by a superior officer, he cannot count on support.

Constable R. mentioned this episode:

The only really dangerous experience I have been involved with taught me several good lessons. It occurred shortly after I started on the job. I was young and quite willing and eager to get involved. On this particular night, I was in a patrol car with another young policeman. A high-speed chase had begun out of our area and out of our precinct. I was driving, so, without permission, I started to go towards the chase. As it turned out the chase turned our way and eventually both cars were coming towards us on R—— Street. I could see the police car in pursuit coming towards us, so I made a roadblock in the middle of the road. The guys in the car being pursued, seeing that the road was blocked, started to slow down and seemed to be coming to a stop. So I stepped out from behind the car and then the car speeded up, went around our car and struck me as I was trying to get out of the way. I learned several things from this experi-

ence. First, I shouldn't act on my own, unless permission or order is given to do so. Second, I should not go out of my district and, in this case, precinct, when the matter at hand was not that grave and could have been handled easily by the unit that was in pursuit. I sure caught a lot of flack for that one, and I deserved it.

Younger policemen, eager to prove themselves, find it difficult to restrict themselves and their operations to the orders handed out. This is one of the major problems facing sergeants who have to see to it that all areas of the city are covered by patrol cars, and it makes their task impossible if over-zealous rookies go off on their own and fail to follow orders. Constable R. discovered for himself that police work involves teamwork; he was nearly killed and, instead of getting a pat on the back for courageous work, he got a severe reprimand. He also learned that his inexperienced definition of the police role was diametrically opposed to the point of view of his superior officer. His wrong evaluation of the situation was quickly and harshly brought to his attention. He was taught how mistaken he was and how dangerous it can be to disobey orders.

In the Courts

Constable M. spoke openly and at length about a difficult episode in his police career:

Learning for the police officer never really ends. He begins to study criminal law at the police college . . . and how to exercise his authority and discretion. When he gets back to the city he must learn the municipal by-laws which are applicable in this particular locality. He must also learn the Police Act carefully because it governs his behavior under a variety of situations. All of this training and learning is necessary and helpful for the new policeman. It is like a frame-work or a structure within which he operates as a policeman. However it is often those unwritten things that are the most important for the individual police officer. People usually learn by imitating others. The same is true for young police officers who generally try to imitate senior officers. At this point in his career the police officer will become a good, mediocre or bad policeman. Early in my own life I had what would have to be described as a violent childhood and often an unhappy one. As a result, quick violence was usually the way that I reacted to crisis situations in order to release anxieties. In my teens this violent release was channelled in sports such as football and later judo competitions. As a very young policeman and actually still on probation, I still had a great deal of trouble with violent releases of anxiety. While on foot patrol one evening, I had occasion to come across a person who was lying down in a car which was still running. My first reaction was to check on this person to see if he was okay. However, when I attempted to arouse this fellow, I was greeted with a hatred for policemen that I had never known before. One thing led to another, until this person kicked me in the groin, at which point I blew my cool and pulled this party out of the car and began to force him onto the ground. As usual this violent self of mine came into play with the result that I hurt this person. Someone called into the police station about it with the result that two senior officers attended the scene. After the situation was explained to them, I realized that I had overreacted in defending myself and that I now had to protect my job, which could be in jeopardy, if this person cried police assault. After talking with the senior constables, we came up with a story that was close to the truth, and, since at this time I wanted nothing more in life than to be a police officer, I stuck to this story. When it came time for the trial, I again had to tell this story to protect my job. As a result, this person was convicted and fined in court but the guilt feelings that I felt about lying to a degree about the incident left me with the firm resolution never to lose my cool again nor would I ever say anything but the absolute truth on the witness stand. I am pleased to say that the insights that I learned from this bad experience have stayed with me up to this very day.

Constable M., acknowledging his mistakes, realized that it was at this very early stage of his police career that he had to decide which way he was going. Being a very big and powerful man with a short temper, he learned that he had to control himself in carrying out his duties or he would be in serious trouble. He realized also that he could not live with himself unless he was honest on the witness stand.

The courtroom is another arena where the policeman comes to grips with the realities of his occupation. As the arresting officer or detective involved in the case, he will be called upon by the Crown attorney to present evidence, and he will be cross-examined by one of the many skilled criminal lawyers in the city. He may work very hard to obtain the right evidence and to present it as honestly and competently as possible. If he lies or obtains evidence by illegal or dishonest means, he has to live with this, knowing that he faces possible discovery and disgrace. If he has an exaggerated view of his role in the administration of justice and cannot bear losing a case, he is going to become a very frustrated man.

There are, basically, three options open to him in terms of reacting to his courtroom experience. First, he can draw a lesson from his poor showing on the witness stand and operate in a more calculated way, collecting information meticulously and wording his presentation in court more carefully. Then, regardless of the outcome of the trial, he can relax a little, knowing he has fulfilled his responsibilities as a policeman to the best of his abilities.

This is more easily said than done, for he may allow himself to get personally and emotionally involved with the case and, perhaps, with the victim.

Secondly, he might see himself as an avenger of wrongs against society. If he does he can be led into using a variety of illegal means to win cases or even to personally inflicting punishment on individuals during the process of arrest and detention.

Finally, he may become embittered and discouraged as he perceives miscarriages of justice in the court system. He will be critical of and disillusioned with some judges, criminal lawyers, and Crown attorneys, but may lack the determination to become a skilled adversary in the courtroom.

Westley explains the policeman's courtroom frustration this way:

> To summarize, the policeman's experience with the courts is one in which he finds an unjust and tiresome chore because of extra time and lack of pay. Because of the defence attorney's interrogations, he often feels that he is being tried rather than the culprit. He is made to play the part of the fool. He is often frustrated in his attempt to make a pinch stick by the political machinations of the courts and the existence of the fix. He tends to lose faith in the course of justice and in obtaining the support of the courts for his judgments. He may feel that the only way in which the guilty are going to be punished is by the police. He has anxieties about the results of court action for, if the prisoner is declared innocent, he, the policeman, may be subject to a suit for false arrest. He sometimes gets great satisfaction from his court appearances, for when he obtains a conviction he has, at once, a sense of having accomplished something and a proof of his own competence. (Westley, 1970:82)

Constable N. responded to courtroom pressure this way:

A crisis situation from which I learned a great deal as a policeman, was one in which a man was threatening another man with a shotgun. My partner and I arrived at the scene and saw the suspect run into his home and hide the shotgun under a mattress. When he got into the home, my partner was jumped by four other persons and the suspect. We both fought with the five persons until assistance arrived, and then all parties were ultimately arrested and charged with assaulting police officers. My learning experience came eight months later when the trial took place. I found that, not only was I expected to fight with five people and hurt nobody, but also, I was expected to outmanoeuvre a top criminal lawyer whose job it was to get his clients off. The approach he used was to make it look as if my partner and I had caused the assault and that when our assistance arrived we were excessive in the use of force in effecting the arrest. It was a long trial, lasting four days. We were expected to remember dimensions of rooms and exact positions of people after eight months. The lawyer was successful, and all charges were dismissed. I learned several things from this experience. I must be more exact and complete in making my notes because many of these cases are delayed for a long time and I have to depend on good notes if I want to have any hope of making the arrest stick and obtain a conviction. I must also learn to deal with the frustration of seeing guilty people released.

Constable N.'s experience illustrates one of the most frustrating aspects of police work. After placing himself in danger in the exercise of duty he sees what he considers to be guilty people released as a result of clever manoeuvres by skilled criminal lawyers and questionable decisions handed down by soft-hearted judges. The inclination is to take the law into his own hands and administer curbside justice. The prescribed response is to become more skilled and observant in his work and to prepare and present airtight evidence. The adversary system in the courts places great pressure on the police; but, in the final analysis, if a city has skilled criminal lawyers it can be an incentive for policemen to be observant, knowing they are going to have to face these skilled people in court. The professional policemen have a grudging admiration for honest and skilled criminal lawyers; they present capable opposition. They dislike and resent only the crooked or shifty lawyer. Policemen learn early in their careers that the courtroom is a tough arena, and they must be equally as ready to lose as to win.

The police cannot always win; most realize this. Some police officers and detectives lie; some cheat; some steal, beg, or borrow admissible evidence. If successful in court, they will be commended; but if the evidence fails, or is shown to be falsified, they will be damned. Honest and competent police and detectives have no great admiration for such co-workers; they see them as so anxious for promotion and success that they will be as unethical as the crooked lawyers they criticize.

Summary

In this chapter policemen have described the ways in which they are made into professionals. They learn daily how to deal with stressful encounters. The schooling is completed when the decisions made outside are reviewed and evaluated inside by peers and superiors.

The same applies to courtroom experience in which they present evidence, explain and defend their actions under cross-examination, discover the kinds of evidence to be collected and recalled, how to present it and, finally, what the judicial system expects of them.

The following chapter examines the policeman as isolated. This reaction on his part is the result not only of the stressful factors of his work world, but also of his perception of the public as being non-supportive, demanding, and critical.

Notes

1. Chapter 8 will develop this point more fully.
2. See Schlossberg (1973) for a detailed presentation of these police coping mechanisms.
3. Crisis situations in this context refer to situations involving danger, potential or actual violence, difficult decisions under pressure. What is a crisis for a rookie may not be one, and probably is not one, for an experienced officer.

Chapter 6

Isolation

The world of the policeman is an apparently contradictory one in which brief moments of intense stress punctuate long periods of boredom, and social isolation co-exists with constant contact with the public. This chapter shows the demands of the occupational role isolating the policeman, and frequently his family, from the community. It also considers how the policeman himself can, and often does, become isolated from his own family and the effect of this on his marriage and on his leisure-time activities. This leads to an analysis of the policeman's intense degree of dependence on his own occupational in-group.

Westley explains why and how the policeman becomes isolated:

> The policeman's involvement in his role is very great; the pension ties him to the job for 20 years. It is a shackle that few are willing to throw off. The job dominates his time. He works eight hours a day, six days a week. He puts in a lot of extra time in the courts. The job disrupts his life. He works on shifts, and, working in this fashion, sleeps when other people work and works when they sleep. He is thus cut off from establishing social contacts with other people. He is emotionally involved in the job. Feeling that the good pinch is a high value, many are willing to spend some of their off hours planning how to present a case in court or attempting to break a big case on their own. The job isolates the man and his family. The disrupting shifts make social participation difficult. The rule of secrecy keeps his family and himself from talking about that in which he is most well-versed and most interested. (1970:144)

Whether this isolation is simply one more result of on-the-job stress or whether it is a contributing factor to that stress is not pertinent here.[1] What is crucial in the life of the policeman is the inevitable interplay that takes place between his work life and his private life. The police explain that this tendency on their part to gradually dissociate themselves from the general public is one of many coping mechanisms they resort to in attempts to avoid needless difficulties.

Although this withdrawal from the public diminishes the harassment they encounter off the job, it may promote the climate of distrust and poor communication between themselves and the public: a vicious circle in which the remedy, although providing temporary respite, ultimately worsens the condition.

"I feel like I'm branded."

The longer the men were in police work and the higher their rank, the more they tended to associate only with other police. One veteran, now retired, pointed out how limited his outside contacts were:

The higher I went in the force the fewer people I'd go out with. I couldn't very well go out with the rank and file once I made sergeant and inspector. I don't feel at home with outsiders and, anyway, who needs the hassle? I have a few beers with the other brass at the Legion. You can't even go into an ordinary tavern in town anymore. There is always some young punk who will recognize you or create a scene. It gets to be a pretty lonely life and really, although my uniform is off, I feel like I'm branded. I've had to deal with a lot of people in my thirty-odd years on the force and many of them are not too happy to see me on "civvy street."

Harassment

Sometimes, once it becomes known that a policeman is living in a certain area, there often follows a form of harassment. Resulting fear for his family and difficulties with the public lead the policeman to try to keep his occupation a secret. Constable R. was extremely bitter about this:

I used to have to live in a housing development geared to income. That was before we got a living wage. As soon as the neighborhood found out I was a cop, their kids went after mine, baiting and beating them up. They would come running home, crying, and it put my wife under tremendous pressure. There were dirty, anonymous phone calls and threats. The women froze my wife out and avoided her in the playground area and wherever they got together. As a result of this really cruel treatment, she was a nervous wreck, and it really shook up our marriage. Finally, we were forced to move away and isolate ourselves. We had to go to a much more expensive area, and there we made a point of steering clear of people. Nobody ever sees me in uniform around the house. Even when I go to a store or supermarket, I keep my eyes wide open. If I see a former client of mine, I tell my wife to go out to the car, and that I'll meet her there. If this guy recognizes me, there might be trouble. I don't want her or the children involved. If they find out she's my wife, they can get at me through her.

The men resented the occasions they were singled out on the street as policemen. They expressed concern about the effect of pressure of this sort on their wives and children. For this reason, the majority of the men had private telephone numbers and they and their wives refrained from any close contact with neighbors. Several mentioned direct threats that they and others had received. One suspected that a recent unsuccessful fire-bombing of his house was criminal revenge. Shots from a passing car have been made at the houses of the deputy chief and of a veteran of the force. The policemen felt that they themselves could handle the dangerous aspects of their work but worried about their wives and children.

To avoid difficulties for themselves and their families, several of the men bought homes in little towns surrounding the city, thus diminishing negative encounters and problems with the people they had to police. They found that the best way to live was to separate their social life and their work life from the neighborhood in which they lived. The fact that many of the wives worked, and so did not generally develop close associations with the neighbors, helped in this.

Even when it comes to leisure-time activity, especially vacation time, the police seek seclusion, away from the public. Some liked to hunt and fish or relax in the northern woods. Many looked upon their golf vacation with other policemen as the outstanding event of the year. Constable M. stated:

I like to get away completely; I really don't care if I get a deer or a moose. It's just so peaceful and relaxing with no one around to bother you. I see and deal with people all the time. I don't travel much except to get to a good fishing lake or a hunting area. Then I really unwind.

Now that wages are better, policemen can afford to live in better physical surroundings, private homes or apartments, where there are fewer incidents of harassment and, as the city grows, there is a greater possibility of anonymity and consequent safety. Most of the men stressed again that they tended to associate with their own occupational group.

Choosing Isolation

The police gave three general reasons for their social isolation. First, it was their own choice. They liked to spend time with other policemen because they shared common interests and enjoyed "shop talk." There was an ease of conversation in a relaxed atmosphere. They were able to unwind among their own kind and not be constantly on guard about what they said. There was a feeling of mutual protection, support, solidarity and trust. They knew what to expect from each other and thus avoided being caught off-guard or taken by surprise.

Secondly, police organization dictated this particular lifestyle. They were always on shift work, involved in overtime work in the courts, or on guard duty. Planning in advance was ruled out by irregular demands on their time. As a result they associated with other men on the force who had similar interests and similar schedules. Sometimes this resulted in their living close to their police friends so they could more readily share leisure-time interests.

Finally, they stayed within their own occupational group because of public pressure. They grew tired of people's complaints against police at social gatherings, just as clergymen complain of being collared by individuals with hard-luck stories. It was a means of avoiding the constant criticism and the feeling of being watched and misjudged. Furthermore, they could be caught off-guard or placed in an awkward position where they might be involved in a scuffle or a more violent scene. Or, they might speak too freely and then be reported back to their superiors for saying or doing something that could jeopardize their careers. All of this makes it difficult to establish relationships of trust with non-police. Inspector L. pointed out:

Gradually all our social, family friendships over the years had dried up because of the nature of my job. I had to put in a lot of overtime and travel. This makes it pretty difficult for the wife to make any plans or arrangements. Just to give you an example: my wife and I get invited to this party. She buys a new dress and has had her hair done—the whole bit. She is looking forward to this for weeks. The very afternoon of the party my superior called me in and told me to pack and go to a distant city to pick up a suspect. To say that she was disappointed is an understatement. I bet she had a strong temptation to cheat on me that night. It must have been pretty frustrating for her. After a while, we just didn't get invited out very much. As a result, I was forced to associate more and more with men on the job. I'd go out and have a few beers or take the wife to various police functions. But every year when we went down south on our holidays, we built up a group of married friends and spent the time with them. We really had a ball, and I never mentioned I was a policeman, nor did I worry about the job.

Detective R. said:

I never indicate my occupation to anyone unless I absolutely have to. It's the best way to avoid any hassle or problems. One night I was working late and went to this party about midnight. I was cold sober, and everybody else was pretty well smashed. This guy got pretty ornery and was blaming me for this and that. I really caught a lot of flack that night and I really wasn't in much of a mood to handle it. I said, "Screw it" to myself, belted down a couple and left. After a while you get tired of it and avoid it. I suppose I should be toughened up enough by now, not to give a shit whether people give you a hard time or centre you out at parties, or even deliberately ignore you. But, yeah, I'm human and it does bother me. No matter how hard an exterior I put on. After a while most of us get the feeling that we cops are all alone.

Once in a patrol car the same point was discussed. Constable A. stated:

No, I wouldn't hide the fact that I was a cop. Of course, I wouldn't broadcast it, either. It isn't fair to the other people. They would all be very angry later, when they found out who I was. They might offer me some hash or some other drug or tell me about some little caper they pulled. That would really put me and them on the spot, to say nothing of the host.

Constable M. disagreed:

I don't want to be constantly hassled by people complaining about tickets and police brutality. Or else they're trying to get this ticket fixed or some other little favor now that they're friends for at least fifteen minutes. I tell 'em I work for the city, but if they persist and finger me, I'd admit I was a cop. I guess we get a bit anti-social and avoid people after awhile just to get away from all the bother. Who needs it? We're getting it on the job all the time. I need a break. I don't want to be a policeman twenty-four hours a day but I guess, in a way, I am.

Relatively younger policemen, with more formal education, usually sought a wider circle of friends from different occupations. They appeared more confident and willing to meet socially with people like lawyers or businessmen. Instead of fearing and avoiding social encounters outside their own peer group, they sought contacts with non-police. Constable J. put it this way:

Now I don't go out a lot with other cops. I used to when I was younger. You had to. I wanted to be in with the guys. Now I'm getting tired of cop talk. I want a fuller life. I want to be accepted, not because I'm a cop, but because I am me. Sure, it's a lot harder. It's so easy to slip into the other way. A lot safer. You know what to expect, and you don't make so many slips. But you don't grow either nor do you learn from others. I see some of these old-timers on the force. That's all they talk about—police work—because that's all they know. Maybe it's the courses I've taken or the travelling I've done; but I'm different now. I want to know about a lot of things and do a lot of things before I die. Pretty soon, we'll be getting retirement after thirty years of service. If I live that long, I'll only be in my early fifties. What will I do? Spend my retirement dreaming of the past and my great police exploits? No way! This is just a job, not my whole life.

This was not a typical statement; how successful Constable J. is in rounding out his social and friendship patterns remains to be seen.

Isolation From the Family: "It takes quite a woman."

In certain ways the policeman is not only isolated from the general public but also from his own family. His work life, his problems on the job, his inability or unwillingness to talk about these matters because of departmental policy or through fear of not worrying her, produce barriers between the policeman and his wife. To spare her the more sordid aspects of the job, or worried that she might leak information about ongoing cases, the policeman denies his wife a part of himself. As a younger officer, he learned to unwind only with the other men and often continued to do this after marriage. Since good communication and time spent together in shared interests are regarded as an important ingredient of a successful marriage, it is not surprising that there is a fairly high divorce and separation rate among the city's police marriages. One administrative official put the divorce rate of the force at approximately sixty per cent. Policemen questioned gave many reasons for this high rate. The most frequently mentioned were: long hours, shift work, inability to communicate with wives about the realities of the job, wives' lack of comprehension when they tried to communicate, and wives' demands on them when they came home tired and tense from the daily grind. The men felt that their wives lived in a world apart and could never really understand. On several occasions the subject was raised with policemen's wives. Rather vehemently Mrs. R. had this to say:

I have a job in town. It's not tremendous, but I meet people and feel somewhat fulfilled. I'm not totally dependent upon my husband for my existence. Most cops' wives don't have any idea about what their husbands are up against. A lot of the ones I know can't seem to keep their mouth shut when he comes home. He's been through shit all day long and doesn't want to listen to her gripes and complaints about the kids and the dog. If she complains a lot, he goes out with the boys to get some peace and relaxation. The more she complains the more he goes out. Eventually, if not sooner, he goes after another woman. He has plenty of opportunities because there are lots of women out there ready, willing, and able. So the marriage breaks up, and the wife still doesn't understand why.

Mrs. H. made this point:

Most of the girls who marry policemen are very young and immature. They're infatuated by the uniform, the physique, the manliness of the cop. They're all crazy about Telly Savalas in Kojak. They figure he's very sexy and are attracted to him almost by his toughness and even his coarseness. They have no real idea of a cop's life or what he really is like. They become terribly disappointed when he can't live up to this "super-cop" image. On TV, cops' wives are rarely shown pinching pennies; but they have to do a lot of this in real life. Instead of finding the daring blue knight and exciting, lustful, wisecracking stud, she sees a very tired, beat, nervous, cranky individual who has been through some awful tough scenes. Sometimes he is fearful and self-doubting but afraid to show it to his wife. So he keeps it all in, and there is a big chunk of him that is closed off to her. This whole effort to keep up the John Wayne image is impossible. Rather than confide in her and admit that he is only a mere human being like everybody else, he relaxes with a bottle but it doesn't really help, especially if he's been involved in some bad fights or shoot-outs. It takes quite a woman to understand and appreciate all of this.

The men were not so blunt. They tended to be protective of their wives.

Because the job is so time-consuming, marriage for a policeman is very difficult. Harvey Schlossberg, a New York policeman-psychologist, points out some of the marriage problems policemen and their wives face:

> I had to make this adjustment every three weeks. These changing hours take a large toll on a man. About seventeen times a year you are asked to change your pattern of sleeping, and eating, as well as your sexual patterns. Police are subject to strange sexual patterns because of this change of hours, and their wives also must get accustomed to the change. The shifting hours bring an added hazard to marriage which holds hazards enough. The average wife's routine is upset when her husband sleeps during the day and she must keep the children quiet, sometimes an impossible task. A wife who feels insecure may look on the late hour as a threat to her marriage if her husband fails to come home after work, seeking relaxation elsewhere. The shift that ends at midnight, when he is still wound up from the excitement of the day and wants companionship and gaiety, is the one that may lead to trouble for both the bachelor and the married Don Juan. There is far more sexual temptation for the policeman than for the average man, for a policeman comes in contact with strangers in the early morning hours, particularly women who are on the town, looking for fun and romance. (1973:47)

The wife is frequently left alone and she may be unhappy unless she also has a job and interests outside the home. Some of the men who had been married for a long time to the same woman felt that they were quite lucky. They were well aware of the problems but said they worked hard at their marriages. They liked working around the house and sharing interests with their wives. Constable M. said:

The wife was beginning to let herself go, not slovenly you know, but putting on weight. I figured she needed a little more attention, so I stuck around home a little more. I made a real effort to listen and to notice little things that I could do for her. She perked right up and since then I've tried to be on my toes a little more. Sometimes you don't know what a good wife you've got 'til it's almost too late.

One constable whose marriage was in trouble felt that a policeman should wait several years before getting married. He would be able to learn the job better and get some of that wildness out of his system. He could make a better choice of a wife then. He felt that the woman should be willing to accept the problems, discomforts and worries of the occupation. The only way was to discuss it thoroughly before getting married so that she would know better what to expect.

Dependency on the In-Group

At the outset of his career, the policeman is a member of an occupational group; his work and the friendships he makes on the job are important to him, but they are not his whole life. But, gradually, as we have seen, the job takes up more and more of his time; he becomes more isolated, and he turns increasingly to his fellow police officers for support. They constitute his occupational *in-group*[2], and he depends on them both at work and off the job. This dependency on his in-group for support is much more intense than in most other occupations except, perhaps, the military. For, like the soldier, the policeman depends on his fellow police officers for physical support in times of stress and danger, and these particular shared experiences create a close bond that often carries over into his personal life. They are a key factor in the "macho" world of the policeman. No one, not even his wife, shares in this intense male world and frequently this bonding creates jealousy and resentment. As one wife, who later divorced her husband, stated:

I keep telling him that he has replayed those episodes with his buddies long enough. That's the only time he seems happy. A beer in one hand, a cigar in the other, and his cronies at his side may be heaven for him, but it is often hell for me, and I bitterly resent it. How do you compete with the whole damn police force?

On the job, this in-group solidarity demands almost total allegiance and dedication. It absorbs his time, his interests, and, seemingly, his whole life.

The more he becomes involved, the more other groups in society (including even his family) come to be regarded as members of out-groups. The more defensive and beleaguered the policeman becomes, and the more he confines his efforts and attention to his occupational role, the more he becomes a prisoner of his occupational choice. He sees the world through the strong lenses of his occupational role. His fellows share the same roles and similar difficulties and reinforce in him the police occupational identity. In time, all his activities and interests are affected and he feels comfortable only behind the walls of the police mind. In a sense he lives within the confines of a total institutional structure.[3] There are similarities between some policemen and some individuals serving life sentences. Both become dependent and comfortable inside the walls of an institution; they come to fear the outside world and dangerous situations they may have to face. The prisoner knows that incarceration has taken such a hold that he would find it difficult to operate or even survive on the outside. Gradually, the policeman too begins to feel safe, relaxed and secure within his own in-group. His job, more or less, forces him to restrict, and finally give up on, outside social contacts. His work always takes him out in public but his encounters are almost totally in the line of duty and are mainly authoritarian, impersonal or negative. This reinforces the impersonal defensive stance that he and his in-group gradually take because the public seldom cares to see beyond the badge and the uniform. "I want to be accepted, not because I'm a cop, but because I am me." This constant negative reinforcement, cold treatment, brush-offs, carping criticisms, in a sense, make the public the policeman's jailer. Even if he would try to liberate himself and to operate freely, he feels constraint and rejection. As Officer L. puts it:

What the hell is the use of trying to explain my job and what it requires to anybody else, including my wife. Unless you live it, you can't really appreciate or understand; and that goes for you, too, professor!

He may try travelling incognito, but maintaining his anonymity and thus his freedom for any length of time is very difficult. The longer he has been immersed in his occupation, the easier it is for members of the public to spot him. The more the policeman detaches and separates himself from the public, the more is he a prisoner of his occupation both physically and psychologically. He becomes uncomfortable with and marginal to the outside social world. To act contrariwise would make him marginal to his occupational role.

As the policeman becomes more isolated from the public and even his family, he depends more on his fellow policemen for his self-image. He may be very efficient and successful as a policeman and gain the respect of his peers and superiors but he often pays a high price for it in his private life.

His wife may become a stranger to him, his children may fear rather than love him and the only social life he knows is "with the boys." Even at mixed parties, he may prefer to create an all-male, all-police enclave within which he feels comfortable. What does he really think of himself? Constable L. revealed the following:

No matter how well I do on the job, I don't really like myself very much because I know that I'm not doing too well as a husband, a father, and a social human being. But what am I going to do? Give it up—hell, no, it's all I know how to do. It's my whole life. I drown myself in my work and score points; after work, I drown myself in my bottle. I'm basically a very lonely man but I put up a hell of a good front. Lately, though, I find that I'm losing interest in the job and not getting along too well with the other guys. If that goes, I've got nothing. Have you read about the "Choir Boys"?⁴ That isn't as unbelievable as you might think. Every police force has a group of choir boys. Some are permanent, core members. The others come and go as they feel the need. Look at all those early retirements and suicides in the police departments. If they had a little happier family and social life, maybe they could handle the horseshit in the department.

Wesley points out how the social isolation and other emotional aspects of the job become very important relative to the self-image:

The isolation, the time allocated, the emotional involvement, make the job a major, if not the most important, influence in the police-man's life. Accordingly, it constitutes an important part of his self. . . . The only refuge is isolation, to make certain that one does not become too friendly with the neighbours. Even so, he cannot escape the continued definition of his role. . . . Finding that he is no longer a Catholic, a house-owner, a father, he becomes a police-man. The role, then, is a large element in the self, and the deep involvement of the self in the role produces a consequent involve-ment of the self in upholding the role. Other men in other occupa-tions can keep their jobs relatively anonymous. The blue uniform going down the street and into the house, the blue uniform in the streetcar and in the restaurant, makes it difficult for the policeman to escape definitions and makes the periods of anonymity relatively scarce. Other jobs do not so completely categorize the man, and the job-holder is likely to be considered apart from the job. The police-man, like the Negro or the Jew, is a stereotype, however, in which the label identifies the morality and the personality. He is more ominous, however, than either, for he carries a gun and a club, and is known to use them. Therefore, for him it is exceedingly difficult to dissociate the set and the role. (1970:145)

Summary

This chapter has illustrated how the policeman's profession brings about the relative isolation of the policeman and his family from the community and, frequently, the isolation of the policeman within his own family circle. These lead to a profound dependence on his in-group which then becomes the dominant factor in the shaping of his self-image.

Chapter 7 will present a tentative portrait—as revealed through common attitudes and behavioral tendencies—of the policeman, who is the end-product of all of the socializing factors which were discussed in Chapters 2-6. We will see what the rookie police learn and how they have been affected by their constant contact with the criminal justice system, the police bureaucracy, and the particular public with whom they deal. The stressful incidents they encounter take their toll; but they also teach them lessons that are cruel, sometimes, but lasting. Finally, as they become more and more isolated from the public and sometimes even their families, they turn to their new occupational family for support and understanding.

Notes

1. See Skolnick, 1966:49-52.
2. Wider than the peer group, the group includes all policemen even those from other jurisdictions.
3. See Goffman's *Asylums* (especially pages 1-24) for an incisive development of this theme. In this discussion the walls are social and mental rather than physical.
4. *Choir Boys*, title of a novel by Joseph Wambaugh which describes in hard-hitting detail the after-hour activities of a group of policemen who hardly resemble the image of choir boys. It is a clever, intentional misnomer.

PART IV

The Policeman

Chapter 7

The Policeman: Responses to the Occupational Environment

Preceding chapters have presented the formative influences that affect the police in the process of socialization on the job. This chapter will outline a composite picture of the police occupational identity through attitudes revealed and behaviors displayed by the police. No single policeman among the hundreds encountered possesses all the characteristics and attitudes presented, nor do all the police react in the same way to pressures. There is a wide variation of personality types within the police force. However the majority shared, in varying degrees, most of the attitudes that will be described.

Skolnick has stressed how police in-group solidarity results in a similarity of outlook on the world:

> All occupational groups share a measure of inclusiveness and identification. People are brought together simply by doing the same work and having similar career and salary problems. As several writers have noted, however, police show an unusually high degree of occupational solidarity. It is true that the police have a common employer and wear a uniform at work, but so do doctors, milkmen, and bus drivers. Yet it is doubtful that these workers have so close-knit an occupation or so similar an outlook on the world as do police. Set apart from the conventional world, the policeman experiences an exceptionally strong tendency to find his social identity within his occupational milieu. (1966:52)

Identification of Attitudes

The formative influences that impinge on the police in the course of their work gradually produce corresponding attitudes. Secord and Backman refer the term *attitude* to certain regularities of an individual's feelings, thoughts and predispositions to act toward some aspects of his environment.

Attitudes, then, have three components: feelings are often referred to as *the affective component*; thoughts as *the cognitive component* and predispositions to act or action tendencies as *the behavioral component* (Secord and Backman, 1964:97-100). Attitudes are only one component of the much wider concept of personality. The main interest of this study was to determine how widely shared were the attitudes among the police.

No attempt was made to measure the intensity of these attitudes since it was felt that this would vary somewhat for each individual policeman.

Attitudes cannot be directly observed; they are a hypothetical construct that must be inferred from verbal expression and/or overt behavior.

Attitudes should be distinguished from opinions. Opinions are beliefs that one holds about some aspect of one's environment in a relatively unemotional way. Attitudes imply the presence of an affective component. What will be a strongly felt attitude for some might only be an opinion for others because of the absence of emotional involvement.

This chapter will first present attitudes that the police commonly have towards various aspects of the criminal justice system whose agents they are, the police department within which they function, and various segments of the public with whom they live and whom they police. The second half of this chapter looks at some of the behavioral tendencies that develop as requirements of the role.

Attitudes: Feelings (*Affective*) and Thoughts (*Cognitive*)

Toward the Criminal Justice System

Capital Punishment: There is a high degree of unanimity among the police as to the need for capital punishment. As one officer put it:

Why should we keep them for years in the slammer? They only come back to haunt you when they get out. I figure my life is worth his. All those bleeding hearts say that capital punishment isn't a deterrent as far as murder is concerned. It sure puts a stopper on the guy who has murdered. He won't murder anybody anymore. It is scary out there if you allow yourself to think too much! Here are all these murderers coming out on the street after a long stretch. Do you think they are rehabilitated? Hell, put them in a position where they are going to get caught and sent back, and they are going to kill, for sure, and it's us that they are going to kill. Those politicians and judges aren't the ones that have to face these guys; it's us, and the fewer of them the better!

Another officer put it this way:

Yes, I'm in favor of capital punishment, you bet your boots I am. If those gutless politicians in Ottawa had to go to murders and armed robberies and wherever there is violence they would be singing a different tune. Why somebody who has deliberately killed somebody should enjoy a long life and at the same time the murder victim is denied his or her life and their children have been denied parents, really escapes me.

This reaction stems from a sense for justice and a desire to reduce the number of dangerous people in society; the fewer murderers walking the streets, the fewer policemen killed or maimed. Murderers have nothing to lose if they kill again except to do more time, something to which they are well accustomed. The concept of rehabilitation, the idea that many murders occur in fits of passion and are seldom repeated, the fact that convicted murderers have a low rate of recidivism when released, all fell on deaf ears. For the police the world is well rid of people who murder other people, moreover, the fear of inevitable execution for murder just might save many a policeman's life.

Constable L. pointed out:

We investigated this call and had to go down in the cellar. There was a detective in plain clothes who had forgotten his flashlight, so he let a uniform cop go first. The fellow gave up without a fight. He had previously killed two people and said that he would have shot the detective, not knowing he was a policeman. He didn't shoot the cop, although he had the draw on him, because he was afraid of swinging. Now they are even going to change that part of the law.

Gun-Control: Considering the police view on capital punishment, it is not surprising that they (generally, to a man) strongly favored tighter gun-control laws. Constable R. expressed his feelings this way:

It is getting a lot more dangerous out there. There are an awful lot of guns in this town, and people are using them more often. It's so easy to buy one. You just walk in and lay down the cash and, presto, you're a big man now and you can kill. It may not happen today or tomorrow but if a guy has one around, and it is handy, chances are he will use it if he is being pushed too far. It ought to be a hell of a lot tougher to get a gun. I suppose we could tighten up the laws but, still, if a guy really wants a piece, he can buy hot ones easily, and I don't mean those peashooter .38's we carry.

Social Workers and Parole Officers: The police generally did not hold social workers and parole officers in very high esteem. They regarded them as "bleeding hearts" who were easily fooled by people and who created all manner of difficulty for the police. Constable R. had this to say about them:

Man, oh man, nobody is going to turn me into a social worker! I'm a cop, not one of those sissified do-gooders. All they do is get in the way and make my work more difficult. Those poor bastards, the parole officers, don't know which end is up. Those cons sweet talk them, put on a good show, and they fall for it most of the time. They think they're doing such a great job. Hell, all they're doing is holding these assholes' hands until some good hoist comes along. They keep arguing for these guys even after we have the goods on them. Those social workers don't solve anything and neither do the parole officers; they're part of our problem, and the sad thing is, the judges are listening to them more and more.

Law Courts & Lawyers: Police were highly critical of judges and criminal lawyers and the way "justice" was dispensed. The courts are becoming revolving doors with the criminals back on the streets by the time the police are back on the next shift. It was discouraging to see again and again the same criminals laughing up their sleeves knowing that they would get light sentences, or perhaps merely probation or a suspended sentence. Constable R., when talking about the courts, stated:

It has almost reached the stage where they are giving medals to the criminal. The judges and the criminal lawyers are often in cahoots. The Crown attorney is not experienced enough. He's overworked, with too many diversified cases. He's up against pros, real specialists. To even the odds, he should be more specialized too.

Officer O. continued:

There is no real interest or follow-through once the arrested person is turned over to the detectives. Our force is too compartmentalized and specialized. When we are called to court to testify we're only warned the night before—there is little chance to prepare and to try and remember accurately what happened. We haven't got the chance to talk to and to co-ordinate our testimony with the purposes of the Crown attorney. The Crown attorneys are overworked and underpaid. We need more of them. Because of the work overload there is a lot of plea-copping. I realize that, once the criminal is apprehended, it is the Crown that judges, convicts and sentences. However, I hate to see it thrown out on a technicality or long delays, during which time the police officer obviously forgets the particulars; the witnesses die, are threatened, or paid off to change their minds; judges are changed to ones who might be more lenient or friendly with the defence attorney. I suppose, when you really get down to it, I have to admire the really clever criminal lawyers. They force us and the Crown attorneys to be a little more professional and on the ball. As far as the judges are concerned, we don't need more of them, but we need better ones who are going to be on the job all day. They should be more efficient and conduct business in the court with more dispatch. They should cut out all that grandstanding by the criminal lawyer.

Some of the younger policemen were extremely resentful of criminal lawyers and alleged that many of them were "pulling crooked deals" to get their clients off. They complained that many lawyers assumed that any good confession presented by the police was obtained by fraudulent means or by physical force.

Some of the police, frustrated at the idea that many criminals get off so easily, would like to take the punishment into their own hands. However, for most, the professional police officer learns to get enough evidence before making an arrest, and he takes pride in presenting a professional case. This does not change their attitude towards judges and lawyers; there is a grudging respect towards the ones considered honest and competent. One night, Officer L. commented:

There is no doubt that the judges can apparently be checked up on and complaints can be laid against them; but the police are at a real disadvantage if they lodge a complaint, especially if the complaint is found out to be not too solid. So as a rule the police are quite leery of the judges and know that if the judges come in cold on these cases instead of having discussed them beforehand with the defence attorneys and so on, there might be a little more relationship between the decision and the evidence. They sometimes find it hard to believe that the decision had anything to do with the case presented. Complaints have been lodged with the Attorney General . . . , and as a result things have improved, and the judges come to court on time, at least for a little while. There should be an automatic review of the judge's record and procedures; but only in an extreme situation would a judge be removed from office. Some go back [to cases tried] from three-and-a-half to five years. Particular questions are asked of the police about an accident which happened five years ago, and it is ridiculous to think that they could remember that long ago when they have so many cases to attend to. The judges and the lawyers sometimes make them look pretty stupid, and they bitterly resent it. It is obvious that something has to be remedied; either we get more judges, or else some kinds of cases should be taken out of certain levels of courts.

Constable P. summed up the frustration of the policeman in his relationship with the judges and lawyers as follows:

You're damned right I'm frustrated! All those lawyers, Crowns, and judges, they all went to law school together. They eat and drink together and pal around together. They try to make a fool out of you in the courtroom. They aren't interested in justice, just the buck. So why should I break my butt all the time when I know the case is going to be thrown out on a technicality? Or, they arrange amongst themselves to have a plea-cop and a reduced sentence. Some of them will even drop the case in the middle because the poor slob can't come up with the dough.

Bail: When it came to the question of changes in the law governing bail the police generally felt that the changes were going to make their jobs just that much more difficult. They were especially opposed to bail for people accused of violent crimes who were, in their eyes, dangerous to the community.

Constable R. had no great enthusiasm for new measures with respect to bail:

It doesn't help us at all; especially now, when a man who commits murder or a robbery is allowed out on bail. He can, and often does, commit a few more crimes before he has to go before the court. He takes a chance that he won't be caught, and then he has more money available for his defence. If we catch him pulling one of those jobs, what has he got to lose? He's going to be a bit more trigger-happy and we're the ones who get shot at, not the politicians.

Toward the Police Department

Innovation and Change: The older policeman opposes radical change in the department and is critical of higher educational requirements for the job. The younger man feels that educational upgrading is inevitable, if not helpful on the job.

For the ordinary policeman, change and innovation mean uncertainty and insecurity. Adjustment to a new, expensive communications centre has been difficult. One sergeant who had been on the force for some time was not so sure that police service had improved to any great extent. All he could see were more men who were tied up with machines and not available for patrol out on the street.

During the research period with the men on patrol a new kind of report-keeping, involving more paper-work, was introduced. One assumes that there were good reasons for this innovation but better preparation for and explanation of this change might have reduced the ensuing complaining and frustration among the men.

The Police Association: The police administration does not always regard the Police Association as a progressive organization. As representatives and protectors of the men's rights, they oppose any changes in the police department that might weaken the gains they have acquired over the years. For such things as increased armament, better cars and motorcycles, or any improvement in hardware used on the job they give whole-hearted support; but the introduction in the downtown precinct of a special 8:00 p.m. to 4:00 a.m. [20:00 to 04:00] car, manned strictly by volunteers, met at first with less than full approval.

It is becoming more evident that the Police Association sees itself in an adversary role with respect to the Police Administration and Commission. In certain situations management wanted certain changes that they felt would improve service and make for better police work. The Police Association saw these changes as requiring more work at the same wages; consequently, they were opposed. Management seems to be adopting the same posture. Modelled, as it is, along semi-military lines, the police administration is not inclined to hand over or to share, in any way, what were previously regarded as strictly management prerogatives and decisions. If a long period of open conflict between the administration and the rank and file is to be avoided, it would seem that both sides will have to change their approaches. At this writing there does not seem to be any evidence that this is happening.

Women Police: Most of the men were opposed to female police because they felt it would weaken this previously all-male fortress and the strong bond that united them. The presence of women everywhere on the job would add to existing tension and create awkwardness; it would inhibit them in their language, in their humor and in the easy-going camaraderie that existed among them. Some of the men, from time to time, would jokingly remark that having a capable and professional woman as a partner would be a decided improvement over some of the dull-witted, paunchy excuses for masculinity with which they were saddled day after day; but in the next breath they wondered about the reactions of their wives and worried about the creation of additional problems for their marriages.

The men also objected to women on the force out of a firm conviction that female police could not withstand the rigors of police life. They thought that it would be very difficult for the men because they would feel that they had to protect the policewomen first, and that this would diminish their effectiveness.

Later on, as women finally did come onto the force, the men had to make rather difficult adjustments. However, they conceded that some benefits had ensued. They came to realize that female police officers were often a calming influence at domestic calls. They were relieved when the female police were with them if a woman was involved in a crime; but they could not readily get over the belief that the women were of little use in violent situations. As a matter of fact, they felt they had to protect her *and* contend with the violence alone. They were convinced that the female officer would not be able to manage in an emergency where physical force would suffice to settle things. One inspector mentioned that this radical change had taken place rather well, considering the nervous anticipation that had preceded it. There was still a great deal of resentment among the men, and there was an insistence that the women had to share all aspects of police work. If they could not take it, then they should choose a different profession. Now that the women have been established on the force, the hiring of new police-women creates hardly a ripple.

Cowardice: The policeman is always being tested, and he knows it. The label he wants to avoid at all costs is that of "being yellow" or a coward. He, himself, will put up with almost any kind of aggravation or difficulty with his partner, except that of unreliability in a tight situation. Rubenstein points out that there is the one unpardonable fault among police, namely cowardice:

> A good cop, in the opinion of a policeman, is someone who is will-ing to go on the street each day and do his job—take people to the hospital, break up fights, make car stops, go to the aid of a col-league in trouble, accept injury, and return to do it all over again—without hesitating to do whatever he must to accomplish his pur-poses. A policeman does not admire another man simply because he makes a numbers pinch or because he locks up a bank robber. Anyone can get lucky or learn how to do dirty work.[1] A good cop does not have to love to fight or hit people; but he must be willing to do both and even risk injury and pain rather than accept defeat. "When I first came on the street, I didn't know nothing. I thought, you wear a uniform and a badge, you got a gun, stick, and jack—who is gonna give you any trouble? Who would want to fight with you? You learn quick," a patrolman said. Every policeman learns to accept in silence much that he dislikes about some colleagues—their indifference, viciousness, dishonesty—but he does not have to keep quiet about someone he considers unreliable or dangerous. Even men who have been around for a long time who become "shaky" are not spared because of sentimental ties. (1973:316-17)

If a policeman has acquired the reputation of not being dependable in difficult situations, he will be avoided and ostracized.

Constable V. stated:

When I hear the radio and there is real trouble I try to be the first one there. I don't want them to think that I'm yellow. I couldn't live among those guys if I thought for a moment that, in their eyes, I was gutless. I'm not talking about being afraid. We just have to overcome that. I'll put up with anything in my partner; he can be a closet-queen, cheating on his wife, you name it—anything. But if I know he won't back me up I'll do anything to avoid going out with him.

There was a guy with me once, and we were sent into an ugly situation. It was hot, and a big angry crowd was creating a disturbance. Something about a guy making it with this other guy's wife, and the whole neighborhood was uptight. I get out of the car and pretty soon I'm surrounded by all these people. I expect my buddy to be behind me. You know where he is? In the car—bug-eyed. I got out of that one by the skin of my teeth but not through any help from that guy. I demanded a transfer to another car as soon as I got back. There was no problem. They get to know these guys pretty quick. It can happen once or twice when you're young and inexperienced because of fright. But it better not happen too often or you're through.

When the question arose as to what officers do to get rid of those they consider to be cowards, they just said that they complained like hell and asked not to go out with them. These "cowards" were usually not fired but moved to another job where they would be working alone.

Corruption in the Department: In this sensitive area, little hard information is volunteered to an outsider, even a sympathetic one. The responses when the question came up, and it did frequently, were uniform. The police conveyed the impression that they considered themselves relatively honest (clean) in comparison to U.S. police forces in the big cities. This manner of responding may have been a measure of self-protection, or it may have been the reflection of what they actually perceived to be graft and corruption. The police stated that there was not much point to compromising their own position by involving themselves in corruption.

There seemed to be no doubt in the minds of these police that the problem of police on the take was really no problem at all. They thought it was sensible to be honest because of public support, good wages, and the security offered by the job. The case of one man who got caught with his hand in the till and was forced to resign came up several times. Constable R. had this to say on the subject of graft:

It would be very easy to take graft on this job; but it's not worth it. This outfit is policed internally but they can't catch everything. I believe that 99.9% of the police are honest; but there are always a few bad apples in every profession. There are a few who are suspect in the area of drugs. But I guess the idea is to give them enough rope and they'll hang themselves. If you want to make some extra cash, there are all those guard-duty jobs on the weekends that you can get assigned to. It's pretty easy money so why go the other route? I'm not going to take a chance on losing this job for a few quick bucks. Once you start, they've got you. We're very aware how high our salaries are in comparison to other occupations.

One night the author went to see the film *Serpico* with a policeman and his wife.[2] The wife was incredulous; this could not be a real depiction of police work. The policeman, however, took it in stride. He had been at it too long to be surprised at anything. He pointed out how, alone, Serpico was trying to go straight in an organization corrupt all the way to the top:

In this city the loner would be the crooked cop. The group pressure is all the other way. It's not that we're more honest, it's just that the system isn't corrupt like it is over there. At least not yet and not to my knowledge.

Use of Force: The use of force is an accepted and integral part of police work. They will use it when necessary; they have come to expect a certain amount of violence on their jobs, and they are reticent to report fellow policemen who are brutal or show excessive use of force because they do not want to be labelled "stool-pigeon." Officer D. was talking one night in the squad car:

No cop will turn in his buddy when it is a question of brutality or questionable use of force. They know they have or will have to resort to it any time in their work. Hell, the time that dude went after me and tried to take me out with his boots, I nailed him with mine and plastered his face all over. I felt no qualms about it at all. It was him or me and I sure as hell wasn't going to tie my hands behind my back and let him knock the shit out of me. I remember one poor cop who just could not stomach the beating that his buddy was giving to this weirdo who had attacked them, and reported his buddy to his superiors. He kept kicking and beating up this guy long after he was subdued. So what happened? Hell, he was almost dead. It's his word against his buddy's. The superiors do nothing because they don't want this kind of trouble. No finks allowed. The word got around and although the men realized what had happened and despised the cop who was brutal—it wasn't the first time—and he had gotten a lot of his partners into needless trouble because he was always looking for a fight—they just froze out the poor sucker who had pulled the plug. Nobody, but nobody, wanted to go out with him, talk with him—anything—he was finished on the force and he knew it. So he finally left.

Sergeants, or higher authorities, commenting on this aspect of police work pointed out that they were well aware of the men who were overly aggressive, who were constantly looking for and getting into fights, and who then laid charges in order to cover up. On the whole, they felt that these men were capable policemen but that they had some serious personal problems. Sooner or later, they expected, the judge would see a pattern and there would not be any way for these men to continue to cover up their misconduct. Schlossberg speaks of his experience of police brutality:

On the job I was learning all about cops, learning there were corrupt cops and there were brutal cops who would beat up men they had arrested, both the innocent and the guilty, to force confessions out of them. The corrupt cop, the brutal cop, did not last long in the department. The rest of us wanted to get rid of him as fast as the public wanted us to. But we wanted to be the ones to dismiss our own delinquents. We didn't like the squealer within, the cop who ran to the press to wash the department's linen. While there are cops who take out their violent feelings on the public, most cops try not to use force if they can capture a crook without firing or hurting him. (1973:69-70)

Once the author remarked that it must be very difficult not to "blow one's cool" on the job and got this reply from Officer W.:

I find the job makes me very tense. Just to give you an example, I had just finished checking out a bunch of stores and garages and dropped into this restaurant to get a cup of coffee for me and my buddy who was out in the car. As soon as I walked into this place this young guy, all dressed up, starts cussing me up and down. They never respect the man, just the sight of the uniform, and it is almost like a challenge, like a red light. So I tell him I don't want any trouble —go out to the car—try to get in—he blocks my way—I go around to the other side—same thing. Finally, I blow my cool and pop him one. He just shrivelled up and almost seemed to enjoy it and then cleared out real fast. But I could have been in trouble for assault, if he laid any charges.

My wife, when I come home, just doesn't seem to understand. I'm all tensed up and just want a little peace and quiet but she goes and lays all her troubles with the kids on me. A couple of times I bruised her a bit. This kind of work is hard on marriages. We should be able to let off steam some way before going home. I brought this book, The New Centurions[3], home and told her to read it, hoping she would begin to understand what I'm up against day after day.

Another time I've kept it in all day. It's hot and sweaty. So I see this car parked in a no-parking area. I'm writing out the ticket, and this guy comes running out and says he's only been there fifteen seconds. Normally, I'd just give him a warning; but I'm fed up here, so I tell him he is breaking the law and keep writing the ticket. He calls me every name under the sun—mother this and so finally I pop him one. He picks himself up, wipes his mouth and clears out. I feel like hell and have to go home to the wife. It's a good thing she was quiet that night.

Officer W. was not proud of the times he lost his temper, and he realized how detrimental this could be for his career and his personal life. Nevertheless, he also believed that any backing-down in situations like the ones he described would only be regarded by the public as a sign of cowardice. If he got this label he felt that he would constantly be tested by every "young punk" in the city who wanted to build up a reputation. What better way for some to gain esteem than to brazenly challenge a policeman, especially if it is known beforehand that he is not likely to fight back. It is, therefore, very functional for a policeman to develop his own reputation for being both willing and able to use controlled force wherever necessary. The better his reputation, the less he is actually compelled to resort to force.

Toward The Public

The Public in General: The typical policeman does not count much on the average citizen to help him nor does he wish to associate too closely with the general public. He believes that the public is only mildly sympathetic to him and that even this limited reservoir of goodwill is drying up. He expects to be confronted with hostile citizens who do not appreciate his efforts and who do not agree with the laws that he is expected to enforce. The lot of a Canadian policeman is not as bad as that of his American counterpart; they felt that there was still some respect and support from the public here but absolutely none in the United States. However, they firmly believe that the social climate is deteriorating. There are many more guns in the city, and they cannot count too much on the public to assist them during stress periods. Constable F. put the matter bluntly:

We are all alone out there. Nobody, but nobody, will come to help us but a fellow-policeman if we get into trouble. We depend on each other very much. Everybody else is an outsider; you can't really count on them when you've got your back up against a wall. The public want to have their cake and eat it. They want lotsa law and order, to be able to walk on the streets safely; but just watch all the crying if we resort to strong-arm tactics or curbside justice, we're in trouble, and the public gets all upset. You're damned if you do and damned if you don't. The safest thing for us to do is keep our nose clean and to ignore a lot. It means less hassle for us; but I think it means that more violence and trouble occurs. But, if that is the way the public wants it, then they shouldn't cry if things gradually get out of hand.

Over the years Constable J.'s attitude towards the public has changed:

Whenever I try to give someone a break, I seem to get it in the neck. Here's an example. We picked up this guy out at the race track. He's very drunk and has no control over his bowels and bladder. I finally get him back to the car, take his keys and send him home in a taxi. The next morning I'm called on the carpet. The bastard has laid a complaint. Claimed I had no right to keep his keys. I could have let him drive and then arrested him for drunken driving. There are times when your common sense tells you to by-pass some regulations and give the public a break but I'm going more by the book now; less hassle. It takes time, but you learn—the hard way.

There is, of necessity, a big difference in the attitudes and approach of police to the public in small towns as compared to big cities. Constable L. observed:

There is a greater need for discretion in small towns because you have to see the same people all the time. When I worked in a small town as a policeman, I used to give more warnings, take the kid around to the old man before lowering the boom on him. In a big city you may never see that person again. It is much more impersonal because you move around a lot in the city, and you seldom really get to know a neighborhood well and the people in it. In any small town you don't come on like gang-busters because the tightly knit power-structure doesn't want anything to change. Our job is to keep the lid on and not to rock the boat. If you don't understand that, wherever you are, you're in for a lot of trouble and no promotions.

Constable F. summed up the policeman's attitude with the following:

We're just a bunch of frustrated blue knights. No matter how hard you work, crime still seems to pay, and they seem to get the good-looking dolls. The others get promotions; nothing really changes. Organized crime thrives. The public just don't seem to give a shit. They don't help the police. They don't thank them. You could easily get discouraged. Everybody needs a pat on the back once in a while. You have to be a very strong man to withstand the constant negative feedback.

The police felt that the highest concentration of trouble and domestic calls were in the public housing areas. Constable J. had this to say about the people there:

They have no goal, they're on welfare, they live like bums. The kids are growing up wild, lazy, but worst of all, slovenly. Within a short time, after they move into some of these brand new places, they're a mess.

He mentioned that it would be a good idea to spread these people around rather than concentrating them in one area; as long as they were not sent to *his* area.

Women: There is little doubt that the police, as a group of relatively young, energetic men, share a keen interest in the opposite sex. Their view concerning women is built into their own self-image. Their attitudes are, for the most part, fairly simple and straightforward; although some expressed a rather sophisticated point of view.

As far as women are concerned, the police officer is less than eager to arrest them because he believes they have a strong inclination to charge him with assault simply to get him into trouble. Constable G. states rather categorically:

I try to avoid any hassle when arresting women. If at all possible, I try not to lay a finger on them. You can't trust them. They'll scream and scratch and kick and then later accuse you of indecent assault. Every time that happens, it has to go through a review board. I always make sure that my partner is there to corroborate my statement; otherwise, I'm in trouble. This is one area where I think we could use policewomen.

All of the police stressed the tremendous number of chances they had to take advantage of women; but the happily married ones insisted that it was like going to the supermarket; they looked carefully but didn't touch the merchandise. Officer W. commented on the availability of women and its impact on family life:

Yeah, there are many reasons why our marriages are a mess: late hours, split shifts, overtime, tensions and frustrations of the job, difficulty of unwinding. We get lotsa propositions; we know where the action is, where the broads go who are bored, or lonely, or who look on the uniform as a challenge. If I really want to get a chick, I tell them I'm married, that my wife is great both in and out of bed, that she understands me and shares in the excitement of my life. Sure as hell, this is a challenge to a lot of these broads, and they practically lay right down in the room for you because you know some of them don't get any kick out of breaking up what is already busted. They want adventure and challenge with a blue knight, so I give it to them.

Many of the men claimed to know some of the local prostitutes; some of them were good sources of information and so were not subjects of frequent arrest. Interestingly enough, it was believed by the police that many of the prostitutes in town were not local women but transients.

Some discussions concerning rape were less than sympathetic towards women. Officer R. had one of the stronger opinions on the subject:

I feel that ninety per cent of the broads lead the guy on and when he goes after her she tries to blackmail him or create problems for him. When that doesn't work, she blows the whistle and cries rape. The use of force is very seldom involved; most cases don't stand up in court. Most broads who blew the whistle were asking for it or at least got what they deserved.

A fairly substantial number of officers had gained sympathetic insight into the trauma sustained by raped women; but they were still very careful about arrest and prosecution because of the number of times, in their experience, that scorned or disappointed women had tried to hurt or coerce men by "crying rape."

Immigrants: The policeman is worried and insecure when he encounters the sometimes strange and different, and he would prefer that people act in what he considers to be a rational and predictable manner. The increased heterogeneity of the city's population makes his work more difficult because he does not know what to expect when confronted by people from widely diverse cultures which are relatively unknown to him. His lack of information about these cultures sometimes makes it difficult for him to understand the actions and motivations of these new residents. A consequence of this is that he tends to be conservative in his views and opposed to immigration policies that could alter dramatically the racial and ethnic make-up of the society and, thus, make his work situation more complex.

In practice, the police were not overly concerned with immigrants. They did not see traditionally immigrant settlements as problem areas. Constable L., a second-generation Italian, had this to say:

I try to treat them like everybody else. Sure, they are noisy and hang around a lot. That is part of their culture back home and you are not going to change it. We try to keep it within bounds. I hand out just as many tickets here as any other part of the city. As a matter of fact, we have less problems with recent immigrants than the people who have been here for generations. The immigrants, especially if they're not citizens, are really afraid of being deported, and their experience with the police back home was often pretty bad. Here in the Italian section the lid stays on because there is still a pretty good family and neighborhood structure. When that breaks down, and it is starting, we're in for more trouble.

Blacks: There was much relatively good-natured banter among the men about race but no evidence of enthusiasm for an increase in black representation on the force. As indicated in Chapter 2, the permanent black population in the city under study is between one and two per cent of the population, but the influx of travellers and tourists creates the impression, especially in the downtown area, of a much larger black population. And too, the fact that blacks have been living in this particular area for over one hundred and fifty years and are fourth- and fifth-generation citizens may contribute to this attitude. The police are well aware of the race question but it is not an absorbing concern to them; the vast majority of suspects and criminals with whom they come in contact are white. Despite this, they still did not like the idea of black men dating white girls. Constable R., who casually mentioned his "enjoyment"[4] of black women, said that he would "whip" his daughter's "ass" if she married a black. Constable S. named a hotel where the blacks were not welcomed, and he felt there was a need for a black-owned tavern and hotel where they could get together.

The police attitude towards blacks mirrored that of the working- and lower-middle-class subculture from which most of them sprang. However they are taken aback by accusations of racism, and they resent the hatred fomented by a few of the men who aggressively harass blacks and other minority groups in the city.

Bikers: Anger and disgust were the most common reactions to the topic of this local subculture. The police insisted that, if people really knew what bikers were like, they would all feel the same about them.

One night, there were a number of bikers in town for the funeral of one of their group. The tension among the police was palpable. The car in which the writer rode frequently passed by the bikers' clubhouse. Inside, the police were convinced, deals relating to drugs, stolen goods, and counterfeit money were being arranged.

Another night there was a strong rumor of a possible fight between two rival clubs and one policeman commented:

They're crazy animals; they all seem to have guns at work and hide them in their lockers. They want to sucker us into a stupid move. We know exactly what they're like and what to expect. Ever since that time at —— when these bikers beat up an off-duty cop and his brother, there has been real trouble. For six months after that we hassled them every chance we got. Things have quieted down a lot since then. You wouldn't believe what their initiations are like. They force the new guys to act like pigs; then they can't go anywhere else; they have to stick together. They're only brave when they outnumber everybody else. If the time came and there was a shoot-out, it wouldn't bother me to plug one of them. The city would be better off without them. There have been lotsa threats around town about getting policemen and their families. They have fire-bombed some policemen's cars. When I stop them, or have anything to do with them, I'm really on my guard. I don't give them an inch. If I did they'd be all over me and my buddies, and the public would suffer.

It appeared that the extremely negative stereotype that they had of the bikers was the product of frequent encounters and stories that have been passed around to the younger men. These latter heightened fear and tension and deepened the universal disgust that they shared concerning this "common enemy." This is a good example of selective perception and attitude formation: all negative actions were noted and reported; negative expectations fed negative perceptions. This, however, is not to deny the reality of some of the behavior reported.

Homosexuals: The older policemen, especially those who had worked in the special investigation division knew the homosexual scene quite well. Since 1969 homosexual acts, in private, between consenting adults, have been legal. If there is solicitation to participate in homosexual acts a charge of gross indecency can be laid. The police still view homosexuals with a jaundiced eye but do not regard them as dangerous. They know their hangouts and their habits, and they recently broke up a ring of homosexuals involving juveniles, some of whom had been blackmailed. Constable R. had this to say about the ring and homosexuals generally:

Maybe those bastards are sick or were deprived when they were young. I don't know all about that psychological crap that makes saints out of these queers. On the whole they don't bother anyone, and we leave them alone as long as they behave and mind their own business. I know most of them from the old days; then we used to check on them in hotel johns and bus terminals. As a matter of fact I kind of feel sorry for them. They're not a very happy bunch. They seem to have that hunted look on their face. But those guys that were going after those underage kids, I don't have too much respect for them. It's funny; they are not all exactly from skid row either. I don't know what I'd do if my kid ever became a fag. I'd be so ashamed I'd want to just roll over and die, or better yet, just vanish.

The police, themselves, were expected never to entertain any doubt as to their own masculinity and total heterosexuality. It seemed to be an expected attitude that they be very appreciative of female flesh and figure. The slightest overt sign of bisexuality, homosexuality, or effeminacy would mean derision and ostracism.[5]

Ex-convicts: Locals who had done time were well known to the police and got little sympathy. When St. ——, a half-way house for ex-convicts was started, the police gave it grudging support; they felt and still generally feel, "once a crook, always a crook." The long and varied files on some of these people simply served to reinforce their attitude. Constable L. argued:

I don't believe they ever really get rehabilitated. Hell, they just make better contacts and try learning how to do it better. The pen is like a crime school. They come out of there bitter and convinced that they will be just a little smarter the next time. Sure, some of them do quiet time if they can, and make up their minds that they are not going back. But they are in the minority. Most of them hang around downtown at those places I showed you. If they are not planning a hoist or some other crime I'd be very surprised. We keep a very close eye on them and there is damn good reason for it, as far as I'm concerned.

One night the patrol car was called to a residence where a man was creating a disturbance. He had been drinking, had driven his car up on the lawn, had relieved himself on the property, and was now vilifying the residents of the house. The police recognized him as a "rounder" and tried very hard to get him to leave quietly; but he then turned his vilification on them, charging harassment. After much time and more talk, the two constables finally got him to park his car, hand over the keys, and then walked him around the block a few times to sober him up. He was then dismissed with a stern admonition to mind his driving, his drinking, and his manners. He went on his way still muttering curses and complaining about the injustice of his treatment. In this situation both officers had shown considerable restraint and had endured considerable stress. Both of them were angry and upset for the next few hours. One of them later said:

I didn't want to charge him because that would mess up his parole. Like most ex-cons he had a chip on his shoulder that has grown heavier while he was doing time. Sooner or later, with his attitude, he is going to get into some more trouble and have to go back to prison. That has been my experience with most of them and I haven't been wrong very often. Basically he needs a lot of counselling; but I doubt that would help him, and most parole officers are too over-worked and easily taken in by these guys. Life to them is a big con game and they just don't change.

Another night the car was dispatched to a bar where several men had been arguing violently. A fight had started, and the bouncer had made his point by shoving a beer glass into the instigator's mouth. As a crowd gathered the police grabbed the trouble-maker and deposited him in the back seat of the patrol car. He kept screaming at the bouncer and several times made as though to get out of the car and go after him again, at the same time making very sure that the police were always between them. Spitting blood and glass and screaming in pain, he cried for his mother and his wife. At the hospital he tried to intimidate the nurses and the intern, but quickly behaved himself when the police intervened. Later, the officers discussed the incident:

That poor creep has done a lot of time. He's been up for rape and beating his old lady several times. Did you hear him crying and screaming? He's as gutless as hell but tries to put on a big front in front of his buddies. They think he's some kind of hero. How can they be that stupid? He got what was coming to him, the loud-mouthed bastard. It's too bad they didn't do a real job on him in the pen. He's going to get it real good some day. Pros, whether they are ex-cons or not, I admire. But these poor punks are all show, just rank amateurs who couldn't carry out a crime without screwing it all up.

Behavioral Tendencies (*Action Tendencies*)

We move now to the *behavioral tendencies* developed in becoming a policeman. They are the behavioral components of attitudes as they were discussed at the beginning of this chapter. These *predispositions to act*, or action tendencies, are inferred, primarily, from the ways in which the policeman acts or says he is going to act.

The typical policeman takes pride in being a member of what he would describe as a group of very capable men. He is a man willing to learn, but this will be primarily from his fellow officers—the ones he admires. He especially admires, respects, and imitates superiors who see themselves as teachers, as leaders of men, and as support in crisis situations. Regulations and procedures laid down by the department are readily accepted once their purpose and necessity are explained.

He believes that he is doing real police work when he is directly involved in crime solving and the apprehension of criminals. As he grows older he resorts less to force in dealing with fights and potentially explosive situations, relying more on finesse and what he judges to be a convincing professionalism.

When on the job, the policeman is confronted with a wide variety of situations, approached always with caution, no matter how innocent they may appear. His reaction, his behavior in action on the street, is determined largely by what he feels is demanded by the situation and by what he feels his peers and his superiors expect him to do. New situations arise continually; but, with experience, what at first appeared to him as very strange comes to be seen as part of a regular pattern, and he is then more prepared to respond. Certain cases, events or problems become routine and standard behaviors are adopted—behaviors that work, that get the job done with as few snags as possible. Certain behaviors come to be seen as valuable and necessary for the policeman, leading to their internalization as behavioral tendencies, or action tendencies or predispositions to act. Most of the police involved in this study displayed a number of these tendencies or predispositions in common.

Acutely Observant: Several times, while on patrol, the police suggested little games to play. The author was asked to tell the things he saw in a particular situation. The police then delighted in pointing out the various details that had been missed. They were very proud of this ability which does not develop without effort and some claimed the ability to remember, easily, faces, licence numbers and the makes of stolen cars. Anything or anybody who was out of place grabbed their attention. Often, on patrol, stops were made in order to talk with groups of young men in various neighborhoods. The police wanted to know the whereabouts of a certain individual and hoped to pick up information about him. They did not always get their information; but later on, in the car, they pointed out who most of these people were, especially those who had had prior contact with the law.

The policemen who appeared to really love their work were almost always on the alert for patterns and behaviors, for details that either fitted or didn't fit the "usual," the "normal." They did not waste time while cruising but thoroughly patrolled an area. They tried various routes to get to the same point, learning the streets and the back alleys. All of this information, they felt, would be useful in the future whenever they were called to a trouble spot. Knowing the streets of the city, its buildings, their operations, and the people in them was as important to them in their work as a doctor knowing and observing symptoms in a patient. They were shrewd observers of people and seemed to be on guard at all times. Even when stopping speeding bikers or taking reports at an accident or a domestic quarrel they continued looking and listening very carefully. They appeared to be casual and matter-of-fact but later in the car they would point out little things they had seen: a torn jacket, swollen knuckles on a biker—evidence of a fight. After a while the researcher began to notice some of these things but never with the expertise of the police.

These powers of observation sometimes pay dividends in helping to avert trouble or in solving serious crime. One officer recalled how he had once been dispatched to the scene of a murder; the neighbors had all been questioned. There were a few clues, but the murder weapon could not be found. The officer looked everywhere and then decided to look in the garbage pail where he found a long knife covered with blood. Fingerprints were taken from the weapon and this led to the solution of the crime. Had it not been for the careful and thoughtful observation of this police officer the garbage would shortly have been taken away and the crime might never have been solved. Rubenstein makes the same point when describing how careful and observant the police are:

> Whatever his purpose, the patrolman carefully and casually checks the terrain as he advances (remember, there is a nothing routine in this business). No such thing as a routine car stop. When you go to sign a store log, look in the window first to make sure that nobody is lying on the floor under a gun, an instructor said. When he enters a store to answer a complaint or to buy a package of cigarettes, he glances through the window before entering. In ghetto neighborhoods, where continuous vandalism and the lack of insurance have forced many businessmen to operate behind boarded windows, the patrolman does not stride in. He lingers at the doorway for just a moment, monitoring the scene by reading the behaviour of the people who are there. (1973:292)

Secretive: The police, initially, and for some time afterwards, were defensive and secretive with the author about their work. It took several years to build a working rapport with the men. The researcher suspects that, in the early stages, he was fed some information, harmless in nature, to test his ability to keep confidences. Even the probationaries and young officers must wait before the more important "departmental secrets" are revealed to them. Since the problem of communication among various divisions and various levels of authority is one of the most frustrating problems of the men, it is not surprising that an outsider will be kept ignorant, in the dark about many matters. Nevertheless, gradually, over a long period of time, the men began to speak about problems within the department. They avoided mentioning names but discussed in detail their main complaints and sometimes their own personal problems. However, when there were many of them together, they seemed to form a solid wall of in-group privacy and reticence.

They were uncomfortable and wary of discussing anything that pertained to specific crimes under investigation; but this is understandable, for such discussion is against departmental regulations and provincial law. Any evidence or information that might affect the investigation or outcome of a case cannot be divulged. Once the cases were settled in court, it was a different matter. The researcher received detailed descriptions of shoot-outs and wild chases, of bizarre domestic scenes and of drug raids and stake-outs. The constables enjoyed talking about the more exciting aspects of their experiences and seemed to derive much satisfaction from describing and explaining what they obviously considered "real" police work. The more experienced men spoke at length about "the criminal element in town." They would point out this particular ex-convict or that one, what crimes he had committed, how long he had been out, his habits, record, and his distinctive characteristics.

Individually, they were not adverse to describing the many ways that minor regulations were broken, and, both in the cars and on calls, they made no effort to hide various minor infractions of the rules. If they did not like or appreciate a particular sergeant or dispatcher they made little attempt to hide their dislike from the author. They shared departmental rumors, old police stories and jokes, and even some of their fears. There was talk of the heightened tension among the police because of the influx of guns into the city. They felt they would be outnumbered and disadvantaged in any shoot-out and wanted to be able to carry heavier calibre revolvers.

However in such matters as police brutality or graft the walls would go up. Most conceded that there were some who were overly zealous in enforcing the law, or possibly had their hands in the till; but they maintained that this was to be expected in any large police force and expressed the conviction that the problem was minimal in comparison with other forces around the country.

Hard and Cynical: One of the strongest impressions conveyed by the police as a group was that of hardness and cynicism. They feel that they must live up to a very tough, masculine image; any display of emotion is regarded as a weakness. They are fearful of being regarded as too emotional and they wish to avoid this label at all costs. Schlossberg stresses that this masking of emotions and the development of a hardened exterior are necessary for survival and its acquisition is crucial.

> I learned that a policeman has to mask any deep feelings that might interfere with being an effective cop. You can't give in to your emotions of fear, grief, disgust, hopelessness, or give way to the visceral reactions that accompany the sight of sudden death on the highway. A cop often has to act tough and uncaring. He has to hide for the moment his sensitivity and tenderness. He moves from crisis to crisis, and if he shows emotion about every incident he will go to pieces. He has to build up a false front, pretend bravado, exaggerate his detachment, because he comes into contact so often with blood, injury, and death. Much of his work is "sided cases" that is, helping the injured and sick. He sees a hurt child and wants to cry. But he has a job to do and cannot indulge in any show of feeling. This in part is what gives the public the impression police are without feeling. A cop does feel, he can't turn off emotions completely, but he tries to cover them up, showing the public only the mask. What this does to the cop emotionally is something else again, as he sees bodies cut out of cars with an acetylene torch, the removal of hands and legs, even heads, from the back seats of cars. (1973:72-73)

Westley concurs as far as police cynicism is concerned:

> The policeman is a cynic. Faced with the duty of keeping people in line, and believing that most people are out to break the law and do him in if possible, he always looks for the selfish motive. The byword is "What's in it for him?" The good action is for the policeman a relative one; it is good insofar as it indicates a respect for the police and an appreciation of the policeman; but it is bad in that it is sure to have a selfish motive. The world for him is a jungle; everybody is looking out for himself and, to use their terms, "out to make a buck." In such a world, self-preservation and success demand that one look out for his own interests and not be "taken in" by the fast-talking advocates of altruism. . . . The police force for him is an island in a hostile community. The interests of the police are his interests through a community assessment of respon-

sibility. He finds himself a partner to crime and brutality, but even for these he finds group support and a collective meaning. The shock of a hostile community absolves their evil and renders an alchemy of integration. Being one with all, against the universe, the rules sink deep. Secrecy, the good pinch, the maintenance of respect, the definitions of the public, the necessity for violence are fused as a defense against hate. They constitute the role of the policeman in its most profound sense. Role involvement being large, they constitute a morality. The job being a way of life, the structure the self-conception. (1970:147-148)

In relaxed moments there was the ready admission that many sights and scenes still proved upsetting. And policemen realize only too well that denial of their emotions could result in mental health problems. Officer L. discussed this question:

Yes, I think I'm gradually getting that way. You know, hard and cynical. It's a part of me now, and I worry about it a lot. I don't think I like what I see in me. The other night I was driving home after my shift and out of the corner of my eye I saw this young boy on a bike drive right into a car. I stopped my car, comforted the child, talked to the driver, and filled out a report as a witness. I called the police and turned the situation over to the policeman on duty when he arrived at the scene. I then went home and had supper with the family as though nothing had happened. It's not that I don't care, but it seems that I can remove myself from the sadness of an accident like this, do very capably what has to be done and move on. I don't think you can turn this off when you are off-duty or even when you retire.

One night two officers with whom the author was driving explained:

We just finished a call downtown where a man had been dead for several days in a hot apartment where the windows were closed. At first we thought he was a black man; but he was white and ripe. This was my twenty-sixth dead-body call and I have gotten pretty used to it. My buddy here lost his biscuits. The smell was pretty lousy. He'll get used to it, but you can't let it reach you. I guess we become a bit like undertakers and doctors in that regard.

Constable F. chuckled:

I think nothing surprises or bothers me on the job anymore. Except when I see a little kid get killed in an accident. I guess it's because I have young children of my own. I was called to the scene of an accident once where a little girl was killed. All that was left was a pool of blood on one side of the road and small box of candies splattered on the roadside. I cried that day. It just got to me. I took a few extra belts of Scotch that night.

The men do not like handling domestic calls. Constable R. had this to say:

You get to know some of them after a while. They call us in, time after time. They need attention, a shoulder to cry on, a referee. They know we can't solve anything but they feel better afterwards, I guess. I don't get involved. I try to see the funny side, if there is one. They make their own bed and can sleep in it. What the hell, I'm not a social worker.

Police who have been in shooting situations, and they are very much in the minority in this city, try hard not to show that it bothers them. One officer, who had been involved in a serious shoot-out with robbers, spoke about it, but only after several drinks. He was bothered and depressed and mentioned dreaming about it sometimes. In speaking this way, he had let down his guard; his image of the hard, cynical cop had been slightly transformed; but he soon recovered and began to crack jokes. His partner was even more upset by the incident because he felt very dissatisfied with himself and his performance. Under extreme stress, he felt that he had not done enough, had not reacted as well as he thought he should, and he kept blaming himself.

In the car and on the job, these men, and others like them, give no indication of this self-doubt and of the traumatic shocks to their emotional systems. Another officer who had been shot in the leg carried the spent cartridge around with him as a reminder. When no other police were around he vividly described the episode, as though sharing and telling would somehow strengthen his resolve. He spoke of his fear when he got back on the job, and he realized how lucky he had been. When another officer arrived it was business as usual with no references made to any prior occasion. It seems to be a very difficult image to maintain, but absolutely necessary, considering the demands of the job. It is only in unguarded moments and only briefly that some of the fears and doubts are allowed to surface.

In whom can they confide? Their wives, their partners, their superiors? Isn't it better to cover up, not to think about it? Constable R:

You can't afford to carry your heart on your sleeve or let down your guard for one instant. They have to feel that you mean business, that you mean what you say. I've got to crack heads on this job and I can't be always worrying and second-guessing myself. I tried to be nice once, and I ended up with a broken nose. The guy took a shot at me because he thought I was chicken. He interpreted my kindness and hesitation as cowardice. I come on fairly strong in those situations now. You have to.

In other words, they feel that the police role demands that a man appear hard and tough; they must present themselves in this manner in order to be obeyed and to stop trouble before it starts. Frequently policemen must physically push and force people; always they must appear as though they will not back down if the occasion requires the use of force. The uniform is not enough to gain the respect of certain segments of society. What counts is the way you wear the uniform, how sure and hard you appear to the public. Their safety, their survival, and the efficient carrying out of their duties, depend on this kind of self-presentation.[6] Can they turn this off and on like a faucet? Some policemen become this way permanently and profoundly. What was initially an exterior role, a mask, or a functional requirement of the job, becomes an integral part of them both on the job and off. Off duty this behavioral tendency is out of place and comes between him and his wife and children.[7]

One way of dealing with this aspect of the role is through what often appears to be very harsh baiting or through what an outsider would tend to describe as rather earthy humor. It is somewhat like the camaraderie of the soldier at the front. One is either toughened up in the process or he gets out. There is no escaping it and, several times in the patrol car, the author was surprised to hear apparently brutal exchanges between partners. It became clear, however, that this was part of an institutionalized and accepted way of letting off steam, of expressing feelings, frustrations, tension, restlessness and emotions that have been submerged for long hours. It indicates acceptance and solidarity; a game played only by men who know, trust, and respect each other.[8]

Impersonal and Decisive: While on the job, the police try to be as impersonal as possible. They try not to get involved personally or emotionally but this is extremely difficult. Constable R., on traffic duty, reported:

I always keep quiet most of the time, and just write out a ticket. They are usually talking a mile a minute and I avoid a lot of hassle and problems by keeping my conversation to a minimum. I approach them with a smile; but . . . [most times] I leave them a little present. They usually quiet down after a while when they see how useless their argument is. I don't mean to say that I give out tickets all the time. Sometimes if they have a really good story, or at least an original one, I give them a break. My job is to enforce the law, not give sermons.

Part of the impersonal approach of the police stems from the semi-militaristic training and procedures of the police force itself. They are accustomed to taking orders, to discipline, to careful inspection, and to getting on with the job. In most instances their area of discretion is severely limited. There are definite forms to fill out and procedures to follow for almost every type of incident or accident. They are warned not to waste any time on calls because they can be needed at any time for emergencies or more important calls. There is also the constant worry about civilian complaints. By acting in a very cool professional manner, the police can keep the encounter with the citizen fairly neutral and give him or her little basis for complaint. This is quite important to them; give the citizen no cause for complaint because everything goes into the policeman's record and affects his career opportunities.

The police are expected and required by their roles to take charge of a situation to which they are called. The author accompanied the police to an accident scene, to a domestic brawl; they took over, ordered people around and settled the issues as well as they could. The public seemed to expect them to do this, and they accepted it, though not always gracefully. On many occasions, at accident scenes, the drivers involved were in heated arguments when the patrol car arrived. As soon as the police moved in, however, they calmed down and if they renewed the argument the police stepped in and put a stop to it. On one occasion, a young girl was found beside a small ditch soaking wet and badly intoxicated. Many people were milling about but nobody had even thought of covering her with a blanket. Quickly, an ambulance was summoned, and the stories of the bystanders were carefully recorded. The girl was covered and carefully placed in the ambulance and taken to the nearest hospital emergency ward. The entire episode lasted no more than fifteen minutes; but it was only when the police came on the scene that anything happened. The people co-operated fully, telling what they knew, but left all decisions up to the police. They seemed calmer when the police showed up and they expected them to know what to do. Some police, whenever possible, took great pains to explain to the public their procedures and the decisions they had made. It was excellent public relations. Apropos of taking charge, Constable R. commented:

As you get older and more experienced you get more reserved, more careful. You case a situation carefully. You don't take as many chances. The most innocent looking situations are sometimes very dangerous. There are a lot of kooks out there and you never know what they are going to do. You just have to be more impersonal. You can't get too involved, otherwise it reaches you and you can crack up. We're the first ones called to a scene whenever there is trouble. That's us, trouble-shooters. We have to be decisive and keep our cool when a lot of times nobody else is. Later on, after our shift, we have to let down a bit before going home, especially if it has been a very hectic night. It has an effect on your family life, certainly; you can't be reserved or formal and professional there. It just doesn't work. My old lady knows how to handle me pretty well. She kids me a lot when I take myself too seriously. I let her run things at home. I'm tired of being in charge, on the job all the time.

Another reason why it is important that the police remain cool and impersonal on the job is the necessity for filing reports which are later scrutinized by their superiors. They know that, if any case is brought to court, they will have to justify their decisions and they count on their own notes and files. The more self-control they can maintain at the time of the incident, the better the chances of their acting in a manner that will stand up in court, of their having proper evidence and of their being able to point to procedures correctly followed. They realize that you can't afford to arrest the wrong individual or fail to get the required evidence. To do their job well the police must maintain their distance from the public and remain in control. If they allow themselves to be carried away by their emotions—fear, anger, resentment—they are in trouble and they know it.

The Suspicious, Sceptical Policeman: Police learn gradually to be very suspicious, sceptical and inquisitive. Every day they are confronted with lying and deceit. As a result they do not accept the normal "obvious" reasons for anything. They are up against con-artists and hustlers and just the ordinary driver who attempts to talk his way out of a ticket. They witness family squabbles where the stories of husband and wife differ markedly. They are aware that most people have a few things they would rather keep hidden and they are seldom surprised when the obvious becomes the unexpected. Constable L.:

Sure, I'm suspicious. You're damn right I am. I'd better be if I want to stay healthy. They'll try to sucker you every time. I always ask myself, "What's his angle? What's he got up his sleeve?" I always approach a car pretty carefully. Yeah, I'm scared. I want to have the jump on him if he is packing a piece. At a domestic you don't know what to expect. One minute the old lady is yelling bloody murder and the next minute she is scratching you.

Whenever the writer went to a restaurant or a tavern with a policeman the latter always "cased the joint" and then took a seat with his back to the wall. Even off duty, he was careful to avoid being taken off-guard. For the police things are seldom what they appear to be. To be wary, to always be on guard, is to stay healthy; never take anything for granted. The unlocked door of a store, a broken window, an abandoned car may be unimportant. To a policeman they are never so because he is usually the first one at a call, not the detective. The patrolman who has the makings of being a good detective is the type of man who likes to work out human puzzles. He wonders, he questions, and he looks beyond the given story.

One night, after travelling along behind an old car, a cruiser pulled alongside at a red light. Constable C., who was new to the force and who was driving, noticed nothing unusual; then Constable L. said:

They look pretty strange in the car, let's pull 'em over. I think they're pretty nervous and trying to hide something.

As they were going across the street to pull into the parking lot, the occupants of the car threw several cigarettes out of the window; they were found to contain marijuana. The girl in the car was underage, while the three boys were much older. They had two cases of beer in the car and were, it appears, headed for quite a party. The older, more experienced policeman, when asked why he had stopped the car, laughed. He said that it was not just a hunch but the result of long years of watching people, looking for any signs, for any indication of trouble. He had been a policeman for quite a while and thought it helped to be somewhat larcenous at times! To be naïve and accepting or trusting on the job are qualities the police can ill afford. Constable R.:

There are all kinds of little games going on all the time and you can't just take things for granted. I wonder how some guys get rich so quick. They come over here without a cent and, before you know it, they're opening a store or restaurant or apartment building. All those big shots in town. Go back in their family history. Lotsa booze-running money, made in the old days. Fortunes—now they are the pillars of society. What do you think of the restaurant I showed you? Hardly an honest guy in the whole joint. I always stop those guys just on general principles. I know they're pulling something, and one of these days I'm going to catch them. How the hell can they afford those clothes and those chicks? I've never seen them working.

In some instances, this tendency reaches the point at which the policeman trusts no one and tends to believe the worst about everyone. The worst interpretation is placed on any action or situation; but this is the coping reaction of a person who fears being made to look the fool and whose occupational activity constantly puts him into positions where this can indeed happen unless he is on his guard. Skolnick stresses that police are trained to be suspicious as part of their role requirement:

> . . . it is in the nature of the policeman's situation that his conception of order emphasizes regularity and predictability. It is, therefore, a conception shaped by persistent suspicion. Policemen are indeed specifically trained to be suspicious, to perceive events or changes in the physical surroundings that indicate the occurrence or probability of disorder. (1966:47)

Rubenstein also emphasizes this aspect of suspicion and its necessity:

> The policeman brings to almost all of his encounters some degree of suspicion and uncertainty. The law formally recognizes that he must assume risks that citizens normally do not undertake and provides him with the means to protect himself. The potential danger

that arises each time he places himself in contact with someone suspected of criminal acts or intentions can be reduced by exercising
his defensive right to assure himself that the person is not armed.
(1973: 271)

In the policeman's daily life the possibility of physical violence is always
present. It may be directed at his own person or that of his partner or of
someone else; conversely, he himself may have to resort to the use of force
in the line of duty. The police are also faced with frequent challenges to
their roles and work—violence, but non-physical. Crowds may jeer and
make offensive gestures and signs. The police are expected to take in stride
this form of assault and attack. This is expecting a great deal of a man, and
this repeated stress takes its toll on the police. One policeman in his late
thirties, who already had had one heart attack, put it this way:

*I stiffen up as soon as I put on the uniform and head downtown. The doctor had
me take my blood pressure at home and just a little later downtown at headquarters, just before I go out; it goes up an average of ten points. I hate to think
what it's like when I go chasing after a hit-and-run or some other call where the
old adrenalin really pumps. This job shortens the life of a lot of our guys unless
they can handle the stress.*

Another young officer stated:

*Yes, sure I'm aware there are a lot more guns out there in the streets. There are
plenty of guys out there who will throw a punch at a policeman. Hell, in one bad
week, just a little while ago, we had four policemen assaulted and injured while
on duty. I try to not let this get to me. It's all part of the job. I keep busy while
on patrol and I suppose in a sense I welcome a call where there might be a little
action. It sure breaks up a long boring night, let me tell you. You learn awfully
early to keep up your guard and, even then, you're going to have to take a few
lumps. It's like professional sports. You would never step on the ice if you worried too much about serious injury. You expect to hit and be hit and you learn to
live with it. If you are badly injured or even incapacitated, well, that's the
breaks. But with us, it's the guns. It is like they have raised the ante. Yeah, I
worry about the guns in the street a lot.*

Officer S. went on:

*Yeah, there are a lot more guns in the city. A lot of dudes with heavy artillery
get caught at the border but a lot of them get through. This drug scene is pretty
rough and they just don't play with guns, they use them. There was a rumor
going around town a while back that there was a bounty of $500 on the head of
one cop for whoever got him. There is an effort to create fear in the police but
it's mostly chicken-shit stuff. You can't get too excited about it or it will get to
you.*

After every shooting in the city, especially if a policeman has been shot, or shot at, there is a heightened tension among the men. One can feel it in the car although nothing directly is said. Officer R. described a wild chase:

We went after some bank robbers and were being shot at before the robbers were captured. My buddy in the patrol car had to be restrained by other police because he would have torn them apart. One of the bullets went through the top of the seat where he had been sitting. Luckily he was crouched down or he would not have had much of his head left. We were both okay immediately after; but it was later on that we both began to shake and sweat heavily. It began to dawn on us how close we had come to packing it in. We need a lot heavier guns to even the odds. Those service thirty-eights are only pea-shooters. Hell, these guys had an arsenal and they were using it.

Constable L. states:

I wish there was some way to relieve some of the frustrations of this job without taking it out on your wife. You seldom get credit for a good arrest. The time I was shot at I didn't feel anything for a little while. Then you start thinking that the little bastard could have killed you. I started to shake and later on I got madder than hell. I was dead if the bullet in this guy's gun hadn't misfired. It was only two weeks later that I really started to react. My nerves weren't so good for quite a while.

One night while on patrol with Officers T. and L. there were several typical calls involving a runaway cat, a barking dog, some kids on a roof, and a couple of domestics. Towards the end of the shift, however, a call came in that an off-duty policeman was in a tavern, and a man was pointing a sawed-off shotgun at him from under a table. The car raced to the scene, but the men were so excited that they drove past the tavern, had to make a complete turn, came back and came to a screeching halt at the door. Other police cars were there already. The gunman was subdued and taken down to headquarters; fortunately, no one was hurt. This episode made up for the previous rather boring calls; but the officers were happy to return to the car. This specific kind of threat is infrequent; but, nevertheless, it does occur.

Sergeant L. pointed out that some violence was the police force's own fault. He was very resentful of frustrated officers who were aggressive and abusive in their dealings with the public. They hurt the image of the force and undo much community relations effort. These types actually generated violence and created needless trouble, not only for themselves, but also for the other police as well. People don't often take the time to look at the name-plate of the policeman who uses unnecessary force on them. Nevertheless, the adoption of name-tags had, apparently, a salutary effect on the more bad-tempered police who could no longer hide behind the anonymity of the blue uniform. Now they could be identified and this led them to be more careful. No policeman wants too many complaints on his record. Rubenstein describes the violent policemen:

> There are policemen who develop reputations among their colleagues as "headbeaters" or "headhunters," but they are relatively rare. The patrolman knows that the stick can be a lethal weapon if applied to the head, heart, throat, or groin. Unless he loses control of himself, which occurs rarely, feels that he is fighting for his life, or has become a vicious person, he avoids swinging his stick overhead. (1973:279)

An average eight-hour shift in a patrol car is long, tedious, and boring. Even though the men believe that the constant patrolling keeps crime down, they all indicated that they would prefer a little more activity to break the monotony.

The younger police, in fact, sometimes apologized to the author for the lack of action. Admittedly, the nights when there was some "real action" were the most interesting and exciting for an observer; but these were infrequent. What do policemen do to break the monotony, especially on the midnight shifts? Sergeant R. had this to say:

In the old days there wasn't so much going on in some districts of the city. In the west end we used to do a little rabbit and duck hunting to fill in the time. Other times we slept a bit. Everybody knew it was going on; but as long as you were around when needed there wasn't much flack. These days some men still are sluffing off. Sometimes they don't report back to the dispatcher for forty or fifty minutes. They are supposed to keep an accurate log of all their calls and a report on the time spent. But it is easy to pad it. We keep moving them around in various districts but it is still pretty boring at times.

Constable R. complained:

I want to be treated as a responsible professional, not like a private in the army with a sergeant climbing up my back half the time. Yeah, sure, we goof off sometimes when things get dull. Don't you get off the point once in a while when things get dull in the classroom?

Some of the police during the course of the night gradually became more tense if there was little or no excitement. Sometimes in the early hours of the morning, they would stop cars for a spot-check but, really, this was done in order to talk to someone, to do something to relieve the boredom. Some would drive at incredible speeds to get to what appeared to be a simple call. Other nights, the author was given tours of the better known 'passion pits" frequented by some of the city's youth. The police would ask for identity cards as proof of age, or they would speak to some of the girls to determine if they were there willingly. Some officers mentioned well-known lovers' lanes where they would turn spotlights on startled couples who then left rather quickly. On hot summer nights they would get out of the car and just talk. As long as they kept in close radio contact they were not particularly worried. When a call came through they usually welcomed it. The older men had seemingly adjusted to this intrinsic aspect of the job and were not disappointed if hours went by without any great activity.

Summary

In this chapter we have seen certain regularities of thought, feeling, and behavioral tendencies that develop in the police as they gradually internalize and adapt to the demands of the occupational role. Generally speaking, they share similar conservative attitudes about various aspects of the criminal justice system with which they are constantly involved. They strongly favor capital punishment, support stiffer gun-control laws and advocate a rigorous system of bail. In the courts, they perceive too much of a "swinging door" type of justice, judges who are too lenient, and too many lawyers who use questionable tactics.

As far as values and practices of the police department itself were concerned the attitudes of the men varied. Most, if not all, seemed opposed to the use of women police. All feared being labelled cowards. They had little respect for the brutal or corrupt policeman; but no one would ever consider reporting these two matters, especially brutality, to higher authorities.

There was a significant difference of opinion among the police when the question of change and innovation arose. The older men were opposed to changes that would affect them personally (e.g. new educational requirements). The younger men were impatient at the lack of innovation and wanted old rules either discarded or changed.

The police do not expect much support from the public. Frequently, the views expressed about the public at large were bitter. The attitudes to women are mixed. In purely work situations, women are threats. The policeman prefers to steer clear of arresting females and dislikes domestic calls which involve women. At the same time they were very attracted to and appreciative of other female contacts and were genuinely protective of their wives. In keeping with their strong "macho" self-image they had only disdain and pity for homosexuals, who represented for them the opposite of the strong masculine role they were trying to live up to. For a subculture like that of the bikers with their style of life, they have universal disgust.

Their attitudes towards blacks are no different from those of the general population. However, they are very aware and leery of the possibility of complaints about discrimination from that small sector of the population.

They know and accept the old immigrant groups but worry about the new ones, especially those whose cultures are very different and unknown to them.

Over the years, as a result of much experience, the police develop certain behavioral tendencies that serve them well while on the job, but which might prove to be inappropriate, counter-productive, and possibly destructive in their individual social and family lives. They become acutely observant men encased in a shell of hardness and cynicism. They have to be impersonal, cool, and collected in their dealings with the public who want and expect them to take charge in tense, dangerous, and troubled situations. Finally they must be ever suspicious and sceptical of everything and everyone lest they be made fools of at the least, or lose their lives at the most.

The following chapter will describe and explain the "occupational identity" of the police which develops as a result of this career-long process of adult socialization into the police occupational role.

Notes

1. For a further analysis of the concept *dirty work*, see Hughes, 1951:313-323.
2. A recent movie about a New York policeman who became aware of chronic police corruption and tried to do something about it.
3. Another police novel by former Los Angeles policeman, Joseph Wambaugh.
4. The term here implies sexual contacts.
5. See Schlossberg, 1973, on this theme.
6. See Goffman, 1959:17-76, for further discussion of this point.
7. See Niederhoffer and Niederhoffer, 1978, for an excellent study of the policeman's family and this theme.
8. Although it sometimes proved painful, the author was grateful when this type of hazing and humor were eventually directed at him. It indicated, at least, qualified acceptance by the subjects of the study.

Chapter 8

The Policeman: Identity Based on Occupation

Concept of Occupational Identity

Earlier chapters have outlined in some detail the main influences within the occupational framework of the police that bring about certain ways of looking at and dealing with the world. The previous chapter, using examples from field notes, advanced a tentative composite picture of the average policeman through his attitudes which have cognitive, effective and behavioral components. A definite indication of a shared police identity emerges. Obviously, there are many individual differences, and no two policemen are exactly alike. Nevertheless, what seems to develop as a result of sharing similar, if not identical, experiences on the job, is what this writer will call an *occupational identity*. This is different from the concept of "working personality" described by Skolnick:

> A recurrent theme of the sociology of occupations is the effect of a man's work on his outlook on the world. Doctors, janitors, lawyers and industrial workers develop distinctive ways of perceiving and responding to their environment. Here we shall concentrate on analyzing certain outstanding elements in the police milieu; danger, authority, and efficiency, as they combine to generate *distinctive cognitive and behavioral responses* in police: a *"working personality."*[1] Such an analysis does not suggest that all police are alike in "working personality," but that there are distinctive cognitive tendencies in police as an occupational grouping. Some of these may be found in other occupations sharing similar problems. So far as exposure to danger is concerned, the policeman may be likened to the soldier. His problems as an authority bear a certain similarity to those of the school teacher, and the pressure he feels to prove himself efficient are not unlike those felt by the industrial

worker. The combination of these elements, however, is unique to the policeman. Thus, the police, as a result of combined features of their social situation, tend to develop ways of looking at the world distinctive to themselves, cognitive lenses through which to see situations and events. The strength of the lenses may be weaker or stronger depending on certain conditions, but they are ground on a similar axis. (1966:42)

In this context, the concept of "personality" appears limited to the occupational environment only. We suggest that, while on the job, a resocialization process takes place, that not only affects the policeman's work, but extends into his private, social, and personal world as well. The degree to which an individual internalizes the occupational role requirements will be partially determined by his basic personality needs.[2] If a policeman finds his needs very well satisfied within his occupational role, then he will be more inclined to develop and strengthen the attitudinal and behavioral patterns most characteristic of that role. If, however, his needs are not being satisfied, he might tend to conform carefully, at least externally, to the occupational expectations of his role, if only to keep a secure, well-paying position.

Policemen can be compared to actors. Some actors are able to step in and out of a role with a minimum of difficulty. Other actors tend to become the role they play. They completely immerse themselves in the role and live it, both on and off the stage. The occupational role of the police is similar. With a prolonged period of exposure to the role and its demands, the policeman, like the actor, must have a strong, well-developed sense of self to be able to discard the role at will. On the basis of this writer's observations, the majority of policemen are not able to do this successfully. Furthermore the policeman is so influenced by the role experience that the occupational identity becomes more and more the "inner core" of that self-identity.

Lefkowitz (1975:19-20), subject to the usual limitations of any such generalization, has indicated that the preponderance of available evidence suggests the existence of a "modal police personality." There are virtually no data to support a conclusion that those modalities are pathological, although some are thought to be undesirable. Thus far, most research on what is called the police personality does not extend beyond the occupational environment of the policeman. The concept of an occupational identity aims to encompass not only the working environment of the policeman but also as much of his personal and social world as possible.

Everett Hughes hints at this possibility:

> The occupational group tends to build up a *set of collective representations* [emphasis mine] more or less peculiar to the occupation . . . the longer and more rigorous the period of initiation

into an occupation the more deeply impressed are its set of social attitudes upon the person. (1971:334-39)

His "set of collective representations" or "set of social attitudes" resembles what this writer means by occupational identity. Because of previously mentioned factors, however, the intensity and pervasiveness of this shared occupational police identity are greater than in most other occupations.

What is being discussed here is the gradual change that occurs in an individual as he becomes a full-fledged member of an identifiable occupation. It is what an individual thinks of himself; what Goffman (1966:105-106) refers to as "ego identity, which is the individual's subjective sense of his own situation and of his own continuity and character, which the individual comes to obtain as a result of social experiences" over time. Upon becoming a member of the police subculture the rookie is gradually socialized into that occupational subculture. He stops thinking of himself as John Smith and identifies more and more with his colleagues and his peers in the work situation. He develops an occupational identity through the internalization of an occupational subculture as expressed by daily interaction and activity with his fellow policemen. He thinks increasingly of himself as policeman and, as the process of socialization continues, he thinks and acts more and more like a policeman. Turner (1971:77) discusses this point, saying "they regard themselves as part of it (the occupation or organization); they regard it as if it were part of themselves. They defend its actions; they rejoice in its success; they identify with it."

With the police this process results in an all-embracing, exclusive and pervasive occupational identity. The original ego identity that the individual brings with him to the police subculture gradually changes over time into this occupational identity. *He is a very different man and thinks and acts both on and off the job according to this police occupational identity.* Few there are, if any, who do not change appreciably or who can withstand the cumulative effects of membership in the police subculture.

Concept of Occupational Identity Applied to Other Professions

The concept of an occupational identity can be applied to other helping or service occupations as well. We may include doctors, nurses, clergymen, social workers and, to some extent, teachers. In many respects they share similar problems and situations encountered by the police.

The characteristics of these service-oriented professions may include some or all of the following:
1) Intensity of involvement
2) Degrees of occupational isolation

3) In-group defensiveness, including job-related humor
4) Surface harshness, cynicism
5) Degrees of social distance; i.e. doctor-patient relationships
6) A focus on the troubled individual: physically, mentally, or morally
7) An "on-call" basis to their occupations, influenced by social expectations.

Although each police officer has different characteristics stemming from his own individual background, there remains a central core of thought, feeling and behavior that is common to all these men. It is not a matter of positing an extreme example of occupational and environmental determinism. This would be simplistic, since each policeman on the force reacts to the demands and trials of his occupation in his own specific way. He learns from and adapts to his fellow policemen, to his superiors and to the general public as he carries out his duties.

Special Factors in the Development of a Police Occupational Identity

The factors that bring about the development of an occupational identity in the police differing from that of the other service-oriented professions may be explained in the following manner. The police are the only ones who can rely on two special resources when performing their duties.

> . . . . The police capability is defined by their special access to *physical force* and *law enforcement* [italics ours] as resources dealing with the problems that confront them. The police licence is their authority to use these two resources.
>
> *Everything* that a policeman does takes place in the context of the police licence and capability . . . the empirical finding . . . does not suggest that the police are "amateur social workers" or "peace officers" rather than "law officers," but that the symbolic presence of the police licence and capability has in most cases enabled the police to deal with the problems facing them without having to resort to law enforcement as a concrete course of action. As the symbolic backdrop of the police licence and capability is always present whenever a policeman responds to a problem, he is always responding as a policeman and not as a social worker, whether amateur or professional.
>
> Indeed the continual presence of the police licence and capability mitigates against him *ever* being able to play the role of social worker as everyone (including the policeman) will know that ultimately he has access to the means uniquely accessible to policemen. (Shearing and Leon, 1977:341-42)

In every encounter with the public, these two resources are always possible means at the disposal of the police. He may not always use them but, nevertheless, they remain in the back of his mind as well as that of the public to be used if all else fails. The public *sees* in *any* encounter with the police the possible use of force or the law, and the reaction is one of apprehension. The policeman *knows* that, in *any* encounter with the public, he may have to resort to force or the use of the law, as coercive, and the reaction on the part of the policeman is also one of apprehension, since there is involved the possible misuse of the licence. Thus every encounter with the public is marked by stress.

The development of the police occupational group identity differs from that of other professions in another way. It takes place primarily in an informal manner on the job whereas in the other caring professions it is more the result of formal intensive training and lengthy preparation. Examples of this may be seen in the clergy, medicine, and to some degree, in teaching and social work.

There seems to be a general consensus among the police encountered in this study that they have learned the most and have been affected the most by their involvement in and reactions to crisis situations in which they found themselves. Over the years there is a similarity in the types of situations, experiences, and problems shared by the police; it seems evident from the data presented that the cumulative effect of these experiences is to socialize or form the individual policeman along common lines. The more limited his non-occupational or non-police contacts are, the stronger will be the impact of his occupation on his outlook. The wider the circle of friends and acquaintances, the more diverse his leisure-time activities, the greater the number of places and countries he visits, the more this will be a countervailing force in his life and the less he will be affected in his thinking and acting by his occupation. But we have seen that the policeman, more than any other professional, is placed in a position of social isolation.

Time is a very important factor in this whole process because the influence or impact on him of his experience is cumulative and affects him in ways that he does not always realize. The policeman's choices are few. If he finds the police world too much for him he can leave. But, if he decides to stay, he has two alternatives: he can either try to live a fuller, more satisfying life by diversifying his leisure time activities and increasing his interests and social contacts; or, he can gradually imprison himself, or allow himself to be imprisoned, within the police environment and find no respite from the job and its powerful influences on him. He will find various rationalizations for his actions, but it is his choice whether or not he will allow himself to become a prisoner of his occupation. No matter how successful or upwardly mobile he may be, the invisible walls of the prison will continue to close in on him. The latter route seems to be the most common one taken among the police. If he lives to retirement he may find himself a stranger in the outside world, a world from which he either fled, or from which he isolated himself for so long.

Notes

1. Italic ours.
2. For further development of this theme see Maslow, 1954.

Chapter 9

What of the Future?

Some Suggestions

The police perform one of the most difficult tasks in our society. There are many aspects of the occupation that are necessary and will not change in the near future. Round-the-clock service and protection requires shift work for the men in this field. Undercover men and detectives are required to work irregular hours as well as doing overtime work in the courtroom. Those who call in sick or who are injured in the line of duty necessitate constant shifting and moving of personnel. To plan, co-ordinate and manage the various aspects of police work requires a large number of administrators, who not only have to organize the work but also see that it is carried out effectively. This requires a hierarchical structure with links of command and increasing responsibility as a policeman rises in the force.

There are, however, aspects of their working environment that can be improved. As a result of this study, some recommendations for possible improvement are presented in this chapter. If they are found worthwhile and put into practice, perhaps some of the unnecessary frustration and debilitating effects of the job could be lessened.

Dispatching Information

One of the most common complaints of patrolmen concerns poor communications within the force. There is often poor radio contact between headquarters and the cars, due to malfunctioning of the radios, or poor vocal quality, or inadequate explanations by the dispatcher. The first is merely a mechanical problem which could easily be remedied. Dispatchers, however, should be chosen with care. Clear voices, good diction, steady nerves and judgment are necessary. If the proper information is not received by the police, or if it is garbled, it can seriously impede their work and even endanger their lives. To strengthen the position of the dispatcher, some police recommended that at least one of them should be promoted to sergeant so that the men in the cars would be less inclined to ignore them or to argue with them.

Sharing Information Among the Shifts

Since there seems to be need for better sharing of information among the various shifts, a shift co-ordinating system might be a possibility. In this system, important information concerning experiences on previous shifts would be relayed to the shift beginning duty. This would be in addition to crime happenings presently given out by the inspector at roll call. Once this is institutionalized, all the men on each shift would be effectively briefed and would be in a better position to do good police work and avoid needless danger or embarrassment.

Sharing Information Among the Officers

There is frequently a lack of communication and information-sharing among the officers. Competition appears to be a major reason for this, despite strict regulations to the contrary. One possible remedy might be to have more of a team approach with both generalists and specialists working together and keeping each other abreast of developments. This would also serve to maintain a high level of personal motivation and a co-operative spirit among the men.

Upward Communication

There seems to be little institutionalized upward communication between the men and officers. In order to avoid gaining the reputation among the officers of being chronic complainers, the constables generally confine their complaints and criticisms to their own group. Patrol officers fear being labelled by their peers as seeking favors from their superiors, and tend to avoid any unnecessary contact with them. The police are modelled along the lines of a semi-military organization. Insofar as feedback and constructive contributions by the "rank and file" are concerned, this model seems to be a poor one. The insights, experience and awareness of the patrolling officers can be a valuable source of information and suggestions. Senior officers who are no longer in the actual patrol situation could benefit from some new system whereby the men could be heard and listened to without fear of recriminations.

Instead of being mainly bargaining units for higher wages and benefits, police associations could improve working conditions and ameliorate situations that are capable of being improved. They would serve as positive channels through which suggestions could be made. This might also result in improved morale among the patrolmen, if they realized what important inputs they could make to the overall police operation.

It is unfortunate that contacts with superior officers fall into basically two categories: reprimands and formal inspections. It is felt that if the men were to meet with their superior officers under less formal circumstances, on a regular basis, an increase in incentive and job performance would surely result. It is also felt, by some officers, that their superiors fear the initiation of positive feedback because it might lead to a breakdown in discipline. They see the superiors as basing order within the department on the fear of being disciplined.

If these areas are not improved, defeatist attitudes will develop among the men who already feel that positive change is difficult if not impossible to achieve.

Recruitment

It should be possible, without lowering standards in any way, to hire more recruits with different cultural and ethnic backgrounds. This would enable the make-up of the force to better mirror the ethnic diversity of the population it serves. A "quota system" according to ethnic percentages in the population is not what is being advocated here. Rather, qualified applicants who are members of under-represented minorities, including women, should be hired whenever possible, but without discrimination in reverse.

Screening Out Potential Misfits

Since very few recruits are hired each year from hundreds of applicants, great care can be, and is taken by those responsible for hiring new personnel to eliminate the obvious psychological and emotional misfits who might apply. Nevertheless, despite the written tests and the challenging oral interviews, it is quite possible that potentially incompetent types might be hired. Psychological testing under controlled conditions is sometimes advocated as a screening device. However, since brutality, dishonesty, and lack of courage and judgment usually make their appearance primarily under stressful conditions, no early screening device is going to be completely effective. What is being advocated is a somewhat longer period of probation during which time the trainees would be more carefully observed. Those who are found wanting should be dropped quietly and speedily. Since police make decisions almost every day that affect the life, health and safety of citizens, the police force cannot be too careful when it attempts to hire and train new police.

Additional On-the-Job Training

Despite the fact that an in-service training program already exists, there is a need for further education and on-the-job training for the police. The following suggestions refer to on-the-job training and have nothing to do with procedures in police colleges or academies. They could help to reduce some of the insecurity and frustration that flow from inadequate information and preparation. As a rookie, the policeman should have experience in a variety of areas. He should work in a variety of precincts and districts. He should also spend some time in the different divisions, thus enabling him to have a better idea of every aspect of police work. He would thus be in a better position, at a later date, to choose an area of specialization that would be to his liking. It would also give his superiors a better basis for assigning him to the type of work for which he has shown the greatest aptitude. The rookie would also have gained contacts in all divisions which would improve teamwork and morale.

Special Reward System

There is a need for a special promotional or reward system whereby good, experienced patrolmen would remain on the street if they liked it and were suited for it, instead of their being shifted to a desk job which they might not handle as well. These men would advance in rank and on the salary scale and would serve as models for the younger policemen on the beat or in the car.

There is a need for personal growth and development on the job, as well as a need for the recognition of that growth. Even at the present time, with all the benefits, the higher wages and better pensions available, many, if not the majority of men, said that they would not become policemen if they had to do it all over again. There are a variety of possibilities whereby the men can improve themselves and become more professional: the study and discussion of special motion pictures for police; acting and role playing (with the aid of a skilled consultant); special days or half-days set aside and run by the police themselves during which they would review problems, cases, situations or mistakes that they have made; the setting up of specialized courses to keep the men abreast of developments in their field.

As the police role becomes a better-paying occupation, higher academic qualifications of applicants can be demanded, with a heavy emphasis on courses that would improve their knowledge of human relations: psychology, social psychology, sociology and political science, law and criminology. If some of these recommendations are implemented the policeman will be better trained and prepared for his job, he will feel there is at least the chance for personal growth within the department and that he will have some contribution to make in the development and improvement of police work. As a result he will develop a better self-image and more confidence. This increased pride in himself as a person and as a policeman would lessen the defensive need to limit his outside social contacts and help reduce his social isolation and its concomitant debilitating effects.

Paraprofessionals

The costs of police protection are escalating all across North America. Because of the costs of a highly educated and professionalized police force, it should be obvious that the talents and skills of these men should be nei- ther wasted nor under-used. As in the health and educational spheres, there is a need for the development of a whole new category of paraprofessionals who could take on the less demanding aspects of police work. A working principle would be to replace a policeman with a lower-salaried paraprofes- sional wherever this could be done without lowering police effectiveness. The introduction of meter-maids is an example of this, and, in some cities, the direction of traffic has been assumed by non-policemen. Certain para- professionals could also be used in the area of crowd control. Para- legal and medical people could be assigned to an emergency squad to handle accidents, to fill out the time-consuming reports, to supervise the restoration of normal traffic, and to administer minor treatment. Some of the paper work and report-writing could be taken over by secretarial help, if better use were made of dictaphones and other more advanced office machinery. Many of the calls dealing with animals should be handled by the Humane Society. With more careful planning and better rapport with other social agencies police would no longer be required to perform many functions that are time consuming and that have little relationship to their skills, training and inclinations.

Knowledge of Social Agencies: Some Human Relations Skills

It is important that the police learn more about the various social agencies and their functions but it is especially important that they have good rap- port with them, since a high percentage of their calls, approximately eighty per cent, are service calls. These calls usually occur at night when most social agencies are closed thus forcing the police to assume, temporarily, a secondary role for which they could be much better prepared.

Workshops presented by representatives of the various social agencies could become an integral part of the policeman's on-the-job training.

Extended Professional Development

In the not-too-distant future, it might be advisable to train a few specialists among the police as lawyers and accountants or in other specialties for the purpose of being better able to combat organized and white-collar crime. Since criminal activities in our society are widespread and more sophisticated it is only common sense that the police should continue to upgrade themselves proportionately if they expect to maintain or increase effectiveness.

Counselling of Policemen's Wives

The policeman's difficult role adds an additional burden to his marriage and, perhaps, counselling and briefing of potential and actual policemen's wives would be in order. In many American cities policemen's wives have joined together and organized to help each other. In New York a trained psychologist (Schlossberg) who is also a policeman is doing good work in study groups with policemen and their wives, helping them to cope with their situation. As a result they have a better idea of what they are going to be faced with in their role as policemen's wives. Some direct contact with their husbands' working environment might be a way of removing some of the TV glamour that surrounds the job.

Difficult or unhappy marriages reduce the effectiveness of policemen who are, themselves, the most valuable component of the police force. Greater effort could be directed towards their group welfare as well as towards such things as the acquisition of more and more technological hardware. The machines and the technology may be very efficient; but if the men operating them are basically troubled and frustrated there will be low performance and ineffective police work.

Public Relations

The police must continue to work at improved public relations. Rather than wait for public outrage and subsequent investigations, they would be well-advised to reprimand and even terminate the employment of men who frequently and regularly create serious problems for the force. At the very least, these men could be encouraged or even required to seek professional help, either on a group basis or individually. Preferably, police departments should police their own organizations and, while respecting the human civil rights of the individuals, they should work out better legal procedures to terminate the service of those police who have proven themselves incompetent. At the present time, once a man is on the permanent force it is very difficult to fire him or to force him to resign. We have seen how the public contributes to the isolation and low morale of the police; it is necessary that the police themselves make an effort to close the gap that exists between the public and the police.

Bill of Rights For the Police

Many policemen across Canada feel that they have fewer rights and less protection than other citizens. This is one of the most important factors contributing to anger, resentment and low morale among the rank and file. It seems to some that, since other minority groups in our society are being protected by Human Rights Codes, the police themselves should be protected by a special Bill of Rights. This bill would assure them of adequate legal protection and due process if they are accused of any impropriety when carrying out their duties. The details of this bill could be worked out by Police Associations and Commissions across Canada.

Civilian Review Boards

With the growing lack of respect for authority and the higher incidence of crime, there is every reason to expect complaints against the police to increase accordingly. Some forces deal with complaints through personnel staff inspectors, higher administration officers and ultimately the police commission. There have been many criticisms of this process by those who wonder if it is possible for the police themselves to adequately investigate complaints and to punish those members found guilty. Advocates of civilian review boards are increasing their pressure to take the entire complaint process out of the hands of police and turn it over to a board made up of civilian members. Civilian boards have been tried in other countries and have met with little success. These boards, because they are composed entirely of civilians, often preclude any possibility of objective justice. Unless the police departments deal more adequately with their wayward members they will find that these civilian boards will be imposed upon them. This is one of the most sensitive areas surrounding the police, but any changes that do take place must ensure the rights of police as well as the public. Already many police have mentioned that they no longer actively seek out crime and criminals; they wish to avoid the inevitable complaints and difficulties that follow. As a result, police protection is diminished, and it is the citizens who suffer. We cannot have it both ways. If the police are going to fulfill their role professionally then those who are breaking the laws or using it for personal gain must be investigated, apprehended and charged. The police will make mistakes, no doubt, but reluctance, on their part, to appropriately exercise their responsibility would be a greater failure.

Epilogue

It is now a few years since the original field research for this book was done. Things have not changed very much, although there are a few more women on the force and a new communications system has been installed. Many of the police from whom I learned a great deal have retired; a few others have died or resigned. However, the factors that create a stressful environment for these men and the newcomers have not disappeared. The individual policemen continue to internalize the role and learn from each other how to survive on the job. It remains the author's opinion that this occupation is one of the most demanding and least understood by the general public. Perhaps the experience of the police I observed is somewhat unique because of the location of the city, but, in reality, the forces at work molding and affecting the police there are similar for every police force in the province.

The size of the city, its location and the make-up of its population may vary from city to city, but the socialization process is the same. One still learns to be a policeman on the street in the toughest classroom of them all; there are no chances to take the examination a second time.

The policeman's role seems to be getting more challenging as the violence in our society increases and the effectiveness of the older institutions, family, church and school, diminishes. In a post-Watergate era, the police are being more carefully scrutinized by members of the press, radio and television. The effect of this adverse publicity is to create an additional form of stress to further strain the policeman's relationship with the public, and to diminish the effectiveness of the men in blue.

Glossary of Terms

artillery, heavy   higher calibre guns (producing more deadly effect)

bikers   motorcycle clubs, some of whose members are involved in crime; outlaw gangs

biscuits, to lose one's   to get sick to one's stomach; to vomit

bleeding heart   idealistic, liberal fighter for underdog—minority rights

blow one's cool   lose one's temper; lose control of situation

blow the whistle   to report someone's mistakes or misdeeds

blue knights   uniformed policemen—adapted from Joseph Wambaugh's novel of the same name; aspect of hero

bucking for promotion   manipulating the system for quicker advancement

case, to   to observe/check out an area or building, usually from a distance, over a period of time prior to entering

cases, sided   cases looked at and put aside because of insufficient evidence to proceed further—instructions are to card and file and place on record

chicken-shit   unimportant minor factor in a situation

closet queen   transvestite (man who likes to dress like a woman)

defuse   calm down a potentially dangerous situation or excited person(s)

disorderly   general term covering calls for police where there is rowdy behavior and drunken fighting, usually at taverns

dogging it   taking it easy; not working too hard

domestic   any call to a home or apartment where there is fighting and bickering—could be very serious and dangerous

finger, to   expose misconduct of peer to superiors; can also mean blame in another context

fink (noun)   a person who lets another person down; undependable person

fink (verb)   to let another person down; to tell on someone

fix, the   pay off for a special favor, as in fixing a ticket

freeze out   to isolate; to give the silent treatment to one who has broken norms of the group

gang bust (verb)   to act aggressively; to come on like gangbusters

gangbusters (noun)   very aggressive people

head beater   brutal or sadistic policeman

hoist   robbery

hot-rodder   fast and often dangerous driver of car or motorcycle

hot shot   person with inflated ego

partners   two officers assigned to patrol in police car for that shift or longer

passion pits   various isolated areas of a city where young couples park in cars and develop their relationship—generally along physical lines!

piece   a gun—usually a small one; a revolver

piece, packing a   carrying a gun on one's person; could also infrequently refer to having it close by, e.g. in glove compartment

pinch, a good   a good arrest

pinch, make a   arrest someone

pinch, numbers   an arrest on illegal gambling charges

plea-copping   arrangement between criminal lawyer and Crown Attorney whereby accused pleads guilty to a lesser charge

plug   shoot someone

pull the plug   to expose someone's misdeeds; to tell someone to hurry

quick on the draw   short-tempered person; does not necessarily mean to use gun

rookie   young, inexperienced policeman—either cadet or 4th-class constable

rounder   an ex-convict or criminal

shoot out   a criminal action, usually armed robbery, where shooting takes place between police and criminals

sluffing off   not working hard; putting in time; not putting one's full energies to work

stool pigeon   a person who tells on another person—usually a small-time criminal who reports to police about other criminal activity

swinging   hanging

take, on the   being involved in graft; being paid a sum of money for not enforcing the law

take (someone) out   to beat up; to render someone ineffective

thirty and out   retirement from police force after thirty years' service

urban cowboy   a city policeman who pictures himself as a modern-day cowboy—violence-prone and inclined to use his gun and club and/or drive his patrol car too quickly

white and right   correctly; along departmental lines

Bibliography

James F. Ahern
1972 *Police in Trouble* (New York: Hawthorn Books, Inc.).
Nicholas Alex
1969 *Blacks in Blue: A study of the Negro policeman* (New York: Appleton-Century-Crofts).
1976 *New York Cops Talk Back: A Study of a Beleaguered Minority* (New York: John Wiley & Sons, Inc.).
Sidney H. Asch
1968 *Police Authority and the Rights of the Individual*, 2nd ed. (New York: Arco Publishing Co., Inc.).
Michael Banton
1964 *The Policeman in the Community* (New York: Basic Books, Inc.).
Morton Bard
1973 "The Role of Law Enforcement in the Helping System," *The Urban Policeman in Transition* (eds.) John R. Snibbe and Homa M. Snibbe (Springfield, Ill.: Charles C. Thomas).
David H. Bayley and Harold Mendelsohn
1969 *Minorities and the Police: Confrontation in America* (New York: The Free Press).
Howard S. Becker
1970 *Sociological Work* (Chicago: Aldine Publishing Co.).
Howard S. Becker and Blanche Geer
1958 "The Fate of Idealism in Medical School," *American Sociological Review*, XXIII, 1 (Feb.), pp. 50-56.
Howard S. Becker, Blanche Geer and Everett C. Hughes
1968 *Making the Grade: The Academic Side of College Life* (New York: John Wiley & Sons, Inc.).
Howard S. Becker et al.
1961 *Boys in White: Student Culture in Medical School* (Chicago: University of Chicago Press).

Howard S. Becker, et al. (eds.)
1968 *Institutions and the Person*; Papers Presented to Everett C. Hughes (Chicago: Aldine Publishing Co.).

Egon Bittner
1970 *The Functions of the Police in Modern Society* (Rockville, Md.: National Institute of Mental Health).

Herbert Blumer
1969 *Symbolic Interactionism* (Englewood Cliffs, N.J.: Prentice-Hall, Inc.).

David J. Bordua (ed.)
1967 *The Police* (New York: John Wiley & Sons, Inc.).

Severyn T. Bruyn
1966 *The Human Perspective in Sociology: The Methodology of Participant Observation* (Englewood Cliffs, N.J.: Prentice-Hall, Inc.).

Hubbard T. Buckner
1967 "The Police: The Culture of a Social Control Agency." Unpublished doctoral dissertation, University of California.

J.V.P. Check and J.F. Klein
1977 "The Personaltiy of the American Police: a review of the literature," *Crime et/and Justice*, 5 (1), pp. 33-46.

Paul Chevigny
1969 *Police Power* (New York: Vintage Books).

Ed. Cray
1972 *The Enemy in the Streets: Police Malpractice in America* (Garden City, N.Y.: Doubleday, Anchor Books).

Robert Daley
1973 *Target Blue* (New York: Delacorte Press).

Jerry Dash and Martin Reiser
1978 "Suicide Among Police in Urban Law Enforcement Agencies," *Journal of Police Science & Administration*, VI, 1.

Richard Daugherty
1970 "The Case for the Cop," *The Ambivalent Force: Perspectives on the Police* (eds.) Arthur Niederhoffer and Abraham S. Blumberg (Waltham, Mass.: Ginn & Co.).

James A. Durner, Mark A. Kroeker, Charles R. Miller and William R. Reynolds
1975 "Divorce—Another Occupational Hazard," *The Police Chief* (Nov.).

Peter Feuille and Hervey A. Juris
1976 "Police Professionalization and Police Unions," *Sociology of Work and Occupations*, III, 1 (Feb.).

John F. Galliher
1971 "Explanations of Police Behavior: A Critical Review and Analysis," *The Sociological Quarterly*, 12, pp. 308-318 (Summer).

Blanche Geer
1972 *Learning to Work* (Beverly Hills, Calif.: Sage Publications, Inc.).
Blanche Geer et al.
1968 "Learning the Ropes: Situational learning in four occupational training programs," *Among the People: Encounters with the Poor* (eds.) I. Deutscher and E.J. Thompson (New York: Basic Books, Inc.), pp. 209-233.
Barney G. Glaser and Anselm L. Strauss
1967 *The Discovery of Grounded Theory* (Chicago: Aldine Publishing Company).
Erving Goffman
1959 *The Presentation of Self in Everyday Life* (Garden City, N.Y.: Doubleday, Anchor Books).
1961a *Asylums* (New York: Doubleday & Co. Inc.).
1961b *Encounters: Two studies in the sociology of interaction* (Indianapolis, Indiana: Bobbs-Merrill Co., Inc.).
1963 *Stigma: Notes on the Management of Spoiled Identity* (Englewood Cliffs, N.J.: Prentice-Hall, Inc.).
Jeffrey Goldstein
1971 "Crisis in Blue: The Police as a Minority Group," *The Other Minorities* (ed.) Edward Sagarin (Waltham, Mass.: Ginn & Co.).
Mr. Justice Campbell Grant
1970 *Commission of Inquiry re Ontario Provincial Police* (Toronto: Queen's Printer, Province of Ontario).
Brian A. Grosman
1975 *Police command: decisions and discretion* (Toronto: Macmillan Company of Canada Ltd.).
Jack Haas
1970 "From Punk to Scale: a study of high-steel ironworkers," Ph.D. dissertation, Syracuse Univ., N.Y.
Jack Haas and William Shaffir
1978 *Shaping Identity in Canadian Society* (Toronto, Ont.: Prentice-Hall of Canada Ltd.).
Richard H. Hall
1975 *Occupations and the Social Structure*, 2nd ed. (Englewood Cliffs, N.J.: Prentice-Hall, Inc.).
Michael F. Heiman
1975 "The Police Suicide," *Journal of Police Science & Administration*, III, 3, pp. 267-273.
Danielle Hitz
1973 "Drunken Sailors and Others," *Quarterly Journal of Studies in Alcohol*, XXXIV, Part A, pp. 496-505 (March).

R. Hogan
1971 "Personality Characteristics of Highly Rated Policemen," *Personnel Psychology*, XXIV, 4 (Winter).

George C. Homans
1950 *The Human Group* (New York: Harcourt, Brace & World, Inc.).

J.R. Hudson
1970 "Police-Citizen Encounters that Head to Citizen Complaints," *Social Problems*, VIII, 2 (Fall).

Everett C. Hughes
1951 "Work and the Self," *Social Psychology at the Crossroads* (eds.) John H. Rohrer and Muzafer Sherif (New York: Harper & Row Pubs., Inc.).
1958 *Men and Their Work* (Glencoe, Ill.: The Free Press).
1962 "Good People and Dirty Work," *Social Problems*, X (Summer).
1971 *The Sociological Eye* (Chicago: Aldine Publishing Co.).

William and Nora Kelly
1976 *Policing in Canada* (Toronto: Macmillan Company of Canada Ltd.).

C.L. Kirkham
1974 "Bitter lessons for a scholar when he dons a police uniform," *The Globe and Mail*, Toronto (May 15).

George Kirkham
1976 *Signal Zero* (Philadelphia: J.B. Lippincott Co.).

Elliott A. Krause
1971 *The Sociology of Occupations* (Boston: Little, Brown & Co.).

William H. Kroes
1976 *Society's Victim—The Policeman* (Springfield, Ill.: Charles C. Thomas).

Joel Lefkowitz
1973 "Attitudes of Police Toward Their Job," *The Urban Policeman in Transition* (eds.) John R. Snibbe and Homa M. Snibbe (Springfield, Ill.: Charles C. Thomas).
1975 "Psychological Attributes of Policemen: a review of research and opinion," *Journal of Social Issues* XXXI, 1, pp. 3-26.

Alfred R. Lindesmith and Anselm L. Strauss
1968 *Social Psychology*, 3rd ed. (New York: Holt, Rinehart and Winston, Inc.).

Michael Lipsky (ed.)
1970 *Law and Order; Police Encounters*, Transaction books (Chicago: Aldine Publishing Co.).

Abraham H. Maslow
1970 *Motivation and Personality*, 2nd ed. (New York: Harper & Row Pubs., Inc.).

L. McV. Mathews
1969 "Chief Reddin: New Style at the Top," *Atlantic Monthly* (March).

George J. McCall and J.L. Simmons (eds.)
1969 *Issues in Participant Observation: A Text & Reader* (Reading, Mass.: Addison-Wesley Publishing Co., Inc.).

John McNamara
1973 "Uncertainties in Police Work: The Relevance of Police Recruits' Backgrounds and Training," *The Police* (ed.) David J. Bordua (New York: John Wiley & Sons, Inc.).

Mr. Justice Donald R. Morand
1976 *The Royal Commission Report into Metropolitan Toronto Police Practices* (Toronto: Queen's Printer).

Patrick V. Murphy and Thomas Plate
1977 *Commissioner, A view from the top of American law enforcement* (New York: Simon and Schuster).

Arthur Niederhoffer
1969 *Behind the Shield: The Police in Urban Society* (Garden City, N.Y.: Doubleday Anchor Books).

Arthur Niederhoffer and Abraham S. Blumberg (eds.)
1970 *The Ambivalent Force: Perspectives on the Police* (Waltham, Mass.: Ginn and Co.).

Arthur Niederhoffer and Elaine Niederhoffer
1978 *The Police Family* (Lexington, Mass.: D.C. Heath & Co., Lexington Books).

Alan Orenstein and William R.F. Phillips
1978 *Understanding Social Research, An Introduction* (Boston, Mass.: Allyn and Bacon, Inc.).

Ronald M. Pavalko
1971 *Sociology of Occupations and Professions* (Itasca, Ill.: F.E. Peacock Publishers, Inc.).

Jack J. Preiss and Howard J. Ehrlich
1966 *An examination of Role Theory* (Lincoln, Neb.: University of Nebraska Press).

R.M. Regoli
1976 "The Effects of college education on the maintenance of police cynicism," *Journal of Police Science and Administration*, IV, 3, pp. 340-345).

Albert L. Reiss, Jr.
1971 *The Police and the Public* (New Haven: Yale University Press).

Thomas A. Reppetto
1975 "The influence of police organizational style on crime control effectiveness," *Journal of Police Science and Administration*, III, 3, pp. 274-279 (Sept.).

Clifton Rhead, Arnold Abrams, Harry Trossman, Philip Margolis
1970 "The Psychological Assessment of Police Candidates," *The Ambiva-*

lent Force: Perspectives on the Police (eds.) Arthur Niederhoffer and Abraham S. Blumberg (Waltham, Mass.: Ginn & Co.).

George Ritzer
1975 *Sociology: A Multiple Paradigm Science* (Boston: Allyn & Bacon, Inc.).
1977 *Working Conflict and Change*, 2nd ed. (Englewood Cliffs, N.J.: Prentice-Hall, Inc.).

Jonathan Rubinstein
1973 *City Police* (New York: Farrar, Straus and Giroux, Inc.).

Harvey Schlossberg and Lucy Freeman
1974 *Psychologist With a Gun* (New York: Coward, McCann and Geoghegan, Inc.).

Paul F. Secord and Carl W. Backman
1964 *Social Psychology* (New York: McGraw-Hill Book Co.).

Hans Selye
1974 *Stress Without Distress* (Toronto: McClelland & Stewart Ltd.).

Clifford D. Shearing and Jeffrey S. Leon
1977 "Reconsidering the Police Role: A Challenge to a Challenge of a Popular Conception," *Canadian Journal of Criminology and Corrections*, XIX, 4 (Oct.).

Edward E. Shev, M.D. and Jeremy John Hewes
1977 *Good Cops—Bad Cops: Memoirs of a Police Psychiatrist* (San Francisco: San Francisco Book Company, Inc.).

Tamatsu Shibutani
1955 "Reference Groups as Perspectives," *American Journal of Sociology*, LX, pp. 562-569 (May).

Allan Silver
1967 "The demand for order in civil society: A review of some themes in the history of urban crime, police, and riot," *The Police* (ed.) David J. Bordua (New York: John Wiley & Sons, Inc.).

Jerome H. Skolnick
1966 *Justice Without Trial* (New York: John Wiley & Sons, Inc.).

David H. Smith and Ezra Stotland
1973 "A New Look at Police Officer Selection." *The Urban Policeman in Transition* (eds.) John R. Snibbe and Homa M. Snibbe (Springfield, Ill.: Charles C. Thomas).

Rodney Stark
1972 *Police Riots* (Belmont, Calif.: Wadsworth Publishing Company, Inc.).

Martin Symonds
1970 "Emotional Hazards of Police Work," *American Journal of Psychoanalysis*, XXX, 2.

1972 "Policemen and Policework: A Psychodynamic Understanding," *American Journal of Psychoanalysis*, XXXII, 2.

Leonard Territo, Charles R. Swanson and Neil C. Chamelin

1977 *The Police Personnel Selection Process* (Indianapolis: Bobbs-Merrill Co., Inc.).

Hans Toch

1973 "Change Through Participation (And Vice Versa)," *The Urban Policeman in Transition* (eds.) John R. Snibbe and Homa M. Snibbe (Springfield, Ill.: Charles C. Thomas).

Barry A. Turner

1971 *Exploring the Industrial Subculture* (London: The Macmillan Press Ltd.).

William W. Turner

1968 *The Police Establishment* (New York: G.P. Putnam's, Sons).

John Van Maanen

1975 "Police Socialization: A Longitudinal Examination of Job Attitudes in an Urban Police Department," *Administrative Science Quarterly*, XX (June).

C.P. Wagoner

1976 "Police alienation: some sources and implications," *Journal of Police Science & Administration* IV, 4, pp. 389-403.

Regis H. Walther, Shirley D. McCune and Robert C. Trojanowicz

1973 "The Contrasting Occupational Cultures of Policemen and Social Workers," *The Urban Policeman in Transition* (eds.) John R. Snibbe and Homa M. Snibbe (Springfield, Ill.: Charles C. Thomas).

Weekend Poll

1978 "Police," *Weekend Magazine*, p. 3 (Aug. 26).

Norman L. Weiner

1976 "The Educated Policeman," *Journal of Police Science & Administration*, IV, 4, pp. 450-457.

William A. Westley

1970 *Violence and The Police* (Cambridge, Mass.: The M.I.T. Press).

James Q. Wilson

1967 "Police Morale, Reform, and Citizen Respect: The Chicago Case," *The Police* (ed.) David J. Bordua (New York: John Wiley & Sons, Inc.).

1970 "Generational and Ethnic Differences Among Career Police Officers," *The Ambivalent Force: Perspectives on the Police* (eds.) Arthur Niederhoffer and Abraham S. Blumberg (Waltham, Mass.: Ginn & Co.).

G. Marie Wilt and James D. Bannon

1976 "Cynicism or Realism: A Critique of Niederhoffer's Research into Police Attitudes," *Journal of Police Science & Administration*, IV, 1, pp. 38-45.

Index

absenteeism, 67
alcoholism, 67
attitudes, 24, 92-93
    affective component, 93
    behavioral component, 93
    cognitive component, 93
Attorney General, 96

Banton, M., 3
Becker, H., 11, 15, 22
behavioral tendencies, 24, 93, 109
bikers, 23, 107
Bill of Rights, 137
blacks, 106
Blumer, H., 6, 10, 14, 23, 25
Buckner, H., 3

capital punishment, 93, 94
Chevigny, P., 2
Chicago School, 25
Choir Boys, 89, 90
civilian review boards, 137
community relations, 121
complaints, 116-117
corruption, 100
cowardice, 99
Criminal Code, 32
crisis situations, 67, 68, 79
Crown attorney, 77, 95

Daley, R., 2
dispatches, 131
distress, 64
domestics, 72-73

empathy, 10
evaluation, 11
expectations, 3

flexibility, 14
fronting, 50, 56

Geer, B., 11
Glaser, B. and Strauss, A., 25
Goffman, E., 56, 90, 124, 127
Goldstein, J., 61
gun control, 29, 94

Haas, J., 11
Hogan, R., 2
Homans, G., 57
homosexuals, 107-108
hot rodders, 38
Hughes, E., 11, 124, 126-127

immigrants, 106
Iowa School, 24
isolation, 3, 82-87

job strain, 64
job stress, 64
job stressors, 64

Kroes, W., 64-65
Kuhn, M., 24

lawyers, 95, 96
Lefkowitz, J., 5, 12, 126
Lindesmith, A. and Strauss, A., 28

malingering, 67
Maslow, A., 130
minority group, 58
Murphy, P., 45, 55

Niederhoffer, A., 12
Niederhoffer, A. and Niederhoffer, E., 124

objectivity, 15
occupational code, 11
occupational identity, v-vi, 2, 4, 9, 24, 88, 92, 125-130
occupational in-group, 87, 90
occupational outlook, 12
occupational role, 2, 9, 10
occupational role-set, 58
occupational subculture, 4
out-groups, 88

parole officers, 94
partial role model, 47
participant observer, vi-vii, 13
peer-group, 12, 42
perceptions, 3
police administration, 98
Police Association, 97-98
police brutality, 101
Police Commission, 98
police identity, 47
police morale, 4
police partner, 44
police probationary, 35-36
police subculture, vi, 4
police turnover, 34
police women, 98

primary relationships, 74
professions, helping, v
promiscuity, 67

racism, 107
rape, 105
recruitment, 133
reference group, 42
Reiss, A., 61
resocialization, v
Rhead, C., 12
role conflict, 44
role expectations, 58
role models, 11, 42, 55
Royal Canadian Mounted Police, 1
Rubinstein, J., 37, 99, 111, 119-120, 122

salary schedule, 34
Schlossberg, H. and Freeman, L., 43, 79, 86, 101-102, 113, 124, 136
Secord, P. and Backman, C., 93
selective attrition, 13
self-selection, 12
Selye, H., 64
Shearing, C. and Leon, J., 128
Shibutani, T., 55
Skolnick, J., 12, 90, 92, 119, 125-126
social agencies, 135
social workers, 94
socialization, vi, 66; occupational, 11
socializing influences, 20
Solicitor General, 1
Stark, R., 2, 12
stereotypes, 2, 3
strain, 64
Strauss, A., 25, 28
stress, 3, 64-67
stressor, 64
survey analysis, 13-19
symbolic interactionism, 9
Symonds, M., 12

Turner, W., 2, 12, 127

Wambaugh, J., 90, 124
Westley, W., 3, 12, 77, 80, 89, 113-114
women police, 98